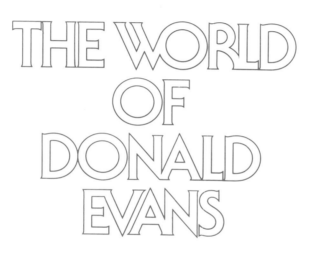

THE WORLD OF DONALD EVANS

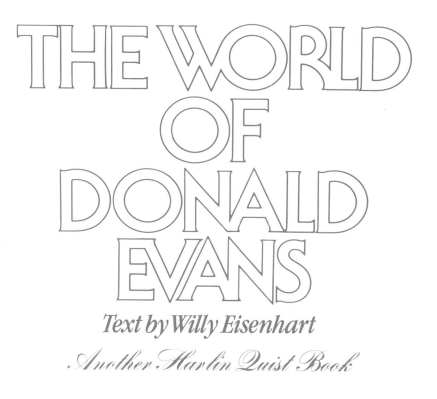

THE WORLD OF DONALD EVANS

Text by Willy Eisenhart

Another Harlin Quist Book

A Harlin Quist Book
Distributed by Dial/Delacorte Sales
One Dag Hammarskjold Plaza
New York, New York 10017

Manufactured in the United States of America
First printing

The book was designed by Patrick Couratin.
The photograph of the artist is by John Vaughan.

Library of Congress Cataloging in Publication Data

Evans, Donald, 1945-1977.
— The world of Donald Evans.

   1. Evans, Donald, 1945-1977.   2. Postage-stamps in art.   I.   Eisenhart, Willy.   II.   Title.
ND1839.E9A4 1980   759.13   80-23652
ISBN 0-8252-9656-0
ISBN 0-8252-9658-7 (pbk.)

For Bill, who blessed it all.

Donald Evans said he liked to be mysterious about his work, but fortunately he was also an inveterate list-keeper. For his watercolors he kept what he called the Catalogue of the World and without its meticulous documentation this introduction to his work would have been impossible. He also made a list of categories of his work as notes for a lecture he gave when he was Visiting Professor of Art at the University of North Carolina at Greensboro in the fall of 1976; this list shows the different ways he thought about his stamps. Its information was invaluable help in choosing the works reproduced in this book.

He also kept an address book. Donald Evans was a gregarious and friendly young man, and he always carried his address book in his back pocket, ready for a new entry. It has about two thousand names of friends in Europe and America, many of them included in the names he used for his stamps. The writer has drawn on his own memories and talked with as many of Donald Evans' friends as time and distance permitted. Information and generous encouragement have come from them and others too: Edward Albee, Andres Amodio, Carol Androfsky, Juan Antonio, Arakawa, Alfredo Arias, Bert Bakker and Yteke Waterbolk Bakker, Joe Brainard, Friso Broeksma, Jon Brunner, Judith Cahen, Remy Charlip, Merce Cunningham, Suzanne Delehanty, Teeny Duchamp, John Duff, Hazel and William Eisenhart, Richard Elovich, Mr. and Mrs. Charles F. Evans, John Evans, Charles Fisk, Suzi Gablik, Victor Garber, Paul Gardner, Madeline Gins, Marilyn Goldin, Larry Hager, Charles and Jan Hinman, Laura Hoffeld, Robert Indiana, Cletus Johnson, Ray Johnson, Jerry Joyner, William Katz, Jolie Kelter, Mrs. Seymour Klein, Louise Lawler, Hitch Lyman, Diana MacKown, Michael Malcé, Patrice Marandel, Marisol, Nancy and Robert McGuire, Herman Menco, Steve Mensch, Christian Murck, Nabil Nahas, Louise Nevelson, Phoebe McGuire Nichols, Walter Nobbe, Claes Oldenburg, Wallace Pinfold, Joan and Joe Potts, Benno Premsela, Erik Roos, Susan Rothenberg, David and Lindsay Shapiro, Hermod Sverre, Xavier Tan, Jonathan Thomas, Gerard van den Boom, Paul van Reyen, Philippe Weisbecker, Nell and Marino Westra, John Willenbecher, May Wilson, Guy Wonder, Rafia Zafar, Barry Zaid and Zeka.

The writer has also relied on the tapes and transcripts generously made available to him of two extensive and invaluable interviews that Donald Evans gave to the editors of the *Paris Review,* George Plimpton, Molly McKaughan and Fayette Hickox; and again to Molly McKaughan, now editor of *Quest* magazine. The published form of these interviews has served the writer as a model for the form of this book.

The works reproduced here will form part of a traveling retrospective of Donald Evans' work that has been chosen, gathered and organized under the auspices of the Stedelijk Museum in Amsterdam by Ad Petersen, curator of prints and drawings. He had first talked with Donald Evans about an exhibition of his work in 1977, and since Donald Evans' death has faithfully and sympathetically seen the project through many vicissitudes to fulfillment with the opening of the show at the Neuberger Museum of the State University of New York, College at Purchase, Suzanne Delehanty, director, in November 1980. The show will then travel to Amsterdam and open there at Christmas 1980 before continuing on tour on both continents.

A book as an accompanying publication to the exhibition was an idea of Donald Evans that found an enthusiastic sponsor in Harlin Quist and his staff: Joni Miller, whose commitment to Donald Evans' work brought about this book; Judy Fireman, the writer's patient and sympathetic editor; Celie Fitzgerald, who wrestled with the production problems; and Patrick Couratin and Gabrielle Maubrie, who solved the problems of design. Jim Harrison bravely acted as copy editor in several languages. Carol Deacon typed the manuscript. David Johnson and John Janzen of Princeton Polychrome Press oversaw the printing, especially the fine full-size color reproductions done with separations made directly from the work.

Donald Evans was fortunate in his dealers. Cora de Vries in Amsterdam, Marilyn Fischbach, Aladar Marberger and Larry DiCarlo in New York, Eric and Xiane Germain in Paris and Hester van Royen in London have helped accomplish this complicated project with advice and information, especially in locating Donald Evans' many collectors. Named and unnamed, they have generously lent their works for many months for study, publication and exhibition.

Donald Evans was an artist and he painted postage stamps, thousands of them. He made these miniature watercolors as a child in his parents' house and as an adult traveling the world. On little paper rectangles he painted precise transcriptions of his life. He commemorated everything that was special to him, disguised in a code of stamps from his own imaginary countries — each detailed with its own history, geography, climate, currency and customs — all of it representative of the real world but, like real stamps, apart from it in calm tranquillity.

The other part of his work is a book in itself, his Catalogue of the World. In it he recorded all his watercolors in a system modeled on real stamp catalogues, including the name of the country that issued the stamps, the fictional date, the subject and occasion of each issue and the date he painted the stamps in parentheses.

This book has been arranged in two parts. First, a short biography introduces the reader to the real world of Donald Evans; second, eighty-five full-size illustrations of his work introduce the reader to the stamps from his imaginary world. There are stamps from twenty-five of the forty-two countries he invented as an adult, and they are arranged alphabetically by country. The accompanying captions tell something of how Donald Evans worked, describe the specific occasions for the work, and explain some of the philatelic devices he used to record the moments of his life.

At 6:40 in the morning on the twenty-eighth of August, 1945, a son was born to Dorothy and Charles Evans in Morristown, New Jersey.

Donald Charles Evans was their first and only child and his mother later told him this story of his birth: the proud parents had been married late in their lives, and Dorothy Evans, a nurse, wanted a son despite several miscarriages and the anticipated risks of childbirth. During another pregnancy, she survived a train wreck, an accident in which many people died before her eyes in an explosion of fire and steam. She felt her survival was a sign that she would have a very special child.

Dorothy Evans had grown up in East Aurora, New York, daughter of a Methodist minister, himself son of the first Methodist minister to cross the Great Divide. Charles Evans, son of a diamond cutter and engraver, had come from Newark, New Jersey, to Morristown and had become a prosperous real estate appraiser. They had bought a house and some land south of the town, between Mount Kemble and the Great Swamp. It was there by Mount Kemble Lake that their son grew up, in what he later called "an ultra-middle-class family."

So concerned was Dorothy Evans for the health of her son that she first showed him to the family relations through the living room picture window. He was a beautiful baby, and once won first prize in the local baby parade. Photographs in the family album show him as a child in paper hats at birthday parties and in a succession of costumes — as the old Fisk tire trademark child with a candle and tire, as a cowboy, an Indian, a chef, Santa Claus and even Uncle Sam. He had stuffed animals (his favorite was Myrtle the Turtle) and he had a dog who once saved his life by tripping him to keep him out of the way of a passing car.

His childhood was idyllic. The house had a big backyard with a swing. Dorothy Evans was a member of the local garden club, and her perfect green lawn was dotted with young trees and bordered with beds of bright exotic flowers and a split-rail fence. Beyond the front lawn, with its light post, yew bush and mailbox, across the narrow road lay a little beach and the lake enclosed by wooded hills.

Donald Evans liked to play outdoors. He learned the flowers' names and he swam in the lake. He was a healthy child, except for bouts of croup, and bright and happy. His parents pampered him and he had everything he wanted.

But there was a perverse streak in him that sometimes showed in stubbornness or tantrums. He wanted to be different, and he liked to play alone. He refused to learn to ride a bike, to play baseball, or to do things that other children did.

And he liked being the only child, objecting outright to his parents' desire to adopt another child.

Donald Evans didn't act his age; he liked to talk with older neighbors. One of them collected stamps and introduced him to that classic educational hobby when he was six. He took to it with a passion. In his room upstairs under the eaves, he pored over his albums of little colored rectangles and he learned about the world. His parents papered his room with maps from the *National Geographic* and he traveled in his imagination to exotic places.

Playing with his stamps, he memorized the capitals of all the countries of the world, all the rulers of Haiti and Hawaii and Tonga, the Friendly Islands — long lists of strange names as well as local customs, money, flags and coats of arms.

There were few boys his own age in the neighborhood, but at school and in the Cub Scouts he made a few close friends. His favorite playmate was Charles Fisk, who lived in nearby Basking Ridge. The mothers arranged for the two boys to play together and drove them to one house or the other.

Donald Evans and Charles Fisk shared practically every interest. They both had their own Myrtle the Turtle, Dinky Toys, piano lessons. Both were introverted, imaginative and uninterested in team sports. Both liked to read and to collect stamps, and both were builders.

On sunny days after a swim in the lake, they took over the beach, each building his own sand castle, adding wings and towers and gates, on and on, each trying to outdo the splendors of the other. On rainy days they built indoors with blocks while their outdoor palaces washed away.

The two boys each invented a character, competing surrogates who commanded the fantastic buildings they made. Charles Fisk came from distinguished old American stock, including an ancestral senator from Massachusetts; his stamp collection was American and so was his imaginary character, Uncle Rich Harvest.

Donald Evans' stamp collection was mainly European and colonial. He was fascinated with Europe and royalty, and he called his character the Queen. The excitement and pageantry of the coronation of Elizabeth II in 1953 led him to mimic the British Commonwealth stamps issued in her honor by drawing his own commemorative stamps for the coronation of his own imaginary queen.

Years later, he told the *Paris Review* he had "had pretensions to better things, what I thought were better things." The Fisks were "well-traveled and had a fascinating house full of collections of things and lots of encyclopedias. [Mrs. Fisk]

DEFINITIVE ISSUE OF 1940

spoke Italian and used to play the piano and sing and we would be playing around the house and I would hear her singing and I thought it was the greatest thing in the world.''

As the two boys grew older, their building became more complicated. They made villages and towns with cardboard houses and cathedrals and highway systems, with soldiers and Dinky Toy traffic. They designed a palace that would collapse with the removal of a single pillar and they staged tidal waves and other disasters, only to begin building again with more elaborate plans. They made maps and calendars and miniature dictionaries and encyclopedias. Their play became as complete and coherent a fantasy as they could devise.

When Donald Evans was ten, he began to concentrate on making stamps. He found he could make the "places more real by making stamps from them and little letters.'' Simultaneously, he was becoming "an obsessive collector of real stamps.'' He awarded prizes to the "stamp of the month,'' his best new acquisition. He studied the designs of real stamps and began to use them as models for the watercolors he painted alone at night — the commemorative stamps of the places he built during the day.

At first, they were crudely drawn and crudely perforated with his mother's pinking shears, but he quickly became more accomplished. He began to outline the stamps in pencil and then fill them in with his pen and brush, and he solved the technical problem of the perforations by pounding out rows of periods on an old typewriter. He gradually transferred the center of his obsession from collecting stamps to making his own, and by the age of thirteen he had stopped building the make-believe towns and villages.

In five years he made a thousand stamps. He invented fifty countries to issue them — places like Frandia, Doland, Jermend, Kunstland (East and West), Slobovia and the Western United Powers. Each had its own flag and coat of arms, currency, government and rulers. Geographies and histories were intertwined with protectorates and occupations, unions and federations. He mounted and identified all the stamps in notebooks — the three-volume World Wide Stamp Album, alphabetically arranged by country. Separately he typed and illustrated leaflets modeled on real collectors' catalogues. For instance, in his "A Catalog of the Stamps of Aluala, 1939-1957,'' he listed all the issues with their dates, denominations and colors as well as prices in Alualan pounds for mint-condition and canceled stamps.

He worked in a stamp store after school and spent his wages on new stamps — he had about one hundred thousand of them — and his range of subjects grew with his collection: varieties of flowers, fruits, trees, fish, birds and animals. He painted landscapes and views of cities and towns, national sports and crafts and national heroes like Washington and Jefferson, Marx and Lenin, Tolstoy, Chopin and Madame Curie. He made imperforate stamps that looked old, with monochrome portraits of rulers crosshatched to resemble engraving, and he made stamps that looked new, with clean modern designs. The cancellations he drew were always appropriate to the period.

He began to research his subjects at the local library and to work from photographs in books, especially his books on cathedrals. (For a school report, "Gothic Cathedrals of Europe,'' he made stamplike illustrations.) He made up his own designs and experimented with different styles of lettering and with different languages. Sometimes he copied out French, German and Russian words; sometimes he simply made them up to sound authentic. He made stamps from Eastern countries with scripts that looked Arabic and Thai.

He began to include his own life in his stamps. He painted portraits of his friends and family, for instance a diptych of the rulers of the Lincoln Isles (its capital is Moorestown) — his royal parents by the lake. When some of Charles Fisk's favorite stamps were stolen from his room at boarding school, Donald Evans commemorated the theft in stamps.

And he began to think about art. He painted stamps of the Mona Lisa and of modern art (abstractions in bleeding watercolor washes). He began to think beyond the single stamp to the composition of a page, like Great Island's Definitive Issue of 1940. He was putting his whole life and everything that interested him into the stamps of his fantasy world — a world he said he tended to like better than the one he was in.

Then at the age of fifteen he stopped. He gave up both collecting and making stamps in 1961; his childhood was over. He told the *Paris Review* he became "less introverted and got involved with people;'' he started going steady with a cheerleader in high school. "I found that people were so interesting. I felt like I couldn't share this stamp obsession with other kids. I got very hung up on being accepted and being like everybody else.'' He began to dress more stylishly, went to football games and set his sights on college. He was over his awkward age and had become a beautiful young man.

Dorothy and Charles Evans think of themselves as "practical, hardheaded and softhearted.'' They value the financial safety and independence of a professional career, and from the start they encouraged their son's talent in architecture.

Donald Evans, however, didn't know what he wanted to do. He later said "the only gut feeling I had was to be an artist but I didn't know what I was ever going to paint if I was an artist. Because I thought to be an artist, you had to be like de Kooning and paint giant abstract expressionist canvases, because that's what people were painting then. This was in the late fifties, just before pop art broke. And I painted big abstract expressionist paintings of the lake. I was starting to smoke then and I wasn't supposed to…and I would go down to the lake and smoke cigarettes and make drawings and then go back and make these abstract expressionist paintings." His work in the new scale was as successful as he could hope; an oil titled *Moonrise* won first prize in a regional competition of students' work.

Donald Evans graduated from Morristown High School in 1963 and spent the summer working as a singing waiter in an Italian restaurant in New Hope, Pennsylvania. He hung around the theater there and thought vaguely about becoming an actor. (He had played the lead in his high school's production of *The Boy Friend*.) In the meantime he painted portraits of friends. And in the fall he went to Cornell University in Ithaca, New York, and decided to study art history.

The next summer he spent wandering Europe (his choice from his parents' offer of the trip or a second-hand car), and then he settled down and followed their advice. In the fall of 1964 he entered Cornell's school of architecture, which he had discovered was quite art-oriented.

A perfectionist and an excellent student, he was determined to be the best at whatever he did, so in the summer of 1965 he took summer courses to make up for lost time. He became skilled at architectural design and won rendering awards. He made the dean's list. He worked summers in architects' offices, in London in 1966, in Boston in 1967, and on a survey of old buildings on Nantucket in 1968.

At the same time, he was always studying art. He took courses in painting and life drawing. He learned to make silkscreens and printed Le Corbusier's "modulor man" on a T-shirt, and he made woodcuts that were sometimes designed to tell stories serially like comic strips. He made large collages and helped stage student "happenings" (one was based on Marcel Duchamp's *The Bride Stripped Bare by Her Bachelors, Even*). He bought a camera and learned about photography, including how to print his own black and white negatives; he made a little leather-bound flip book of photographs of a new friend, Phoebe McGuire. He developed his handwriting, both print and script. He carved erasers into rubber stamps. He even learned to dye and weave.

Phoebe McGuire said they "went to the movies, met people, walked and went to parties." Their friends saw them as a sophisticated, witty and beautiful couple, characters out of an English novel. He was fascinated by her and by her family, so different from his own. Her parents collected antiques and traveled in Europe; her father taught English and her mother made sculpture (and kept a catalogue of her work). Donald Evans shared the McGuire family's interests and traveled with them in England in 1966. (For his birthday he and Phoebe McGuire even tried to go to Lundy, the island "kingdom" off the English coast that issues its own stamps, but the trip was prevented by a storm.) He loved traveling in Europe and realizing his childhood dreams about faraway places. He studied the architectural monuments and visited the great collections, at first with sketchbook in hand, later with his camera.

Besides learning the techniques and the history of art and architecture, Donald Evans learned about contemporary artists. He became friendly with the painter Jim Dine, who was a visiting critic at Cornell. Donald Evans and Phoebe McGuire went to New York and investigated the "scene." Through the poet Gerard Malanga they met Andy Warhol at the Factory, and they went to the opening of the discotheque, the Exploding Plastic Inevitable. Donald Evans even impersonated Andy Warhol at a reading at Cornell and went to a beaux arts ball carrying a Brillo box. On a class trip in New York with his teacher, the painter Charles Hinman, he made friends with Robert Indiana and his assistant William Katz.

He became interested in Experiments in Art and Technology (E.A.T.) and its efforts to encourage collaboration between artists and scientists. For a materials class project, he had the idea to figure out how to build Claes Oldenburg's proposed monument for the intersection of Canal Street and Broadway in New York: a colossal block of concrete inscribed with the names of war heroes. (Its estimated mass of five hundred million pounds would have completely blocked traffic in lower Manhattan.) Claes Oldenburg was delighted to meet Donald Evans, who was the first to take his projects for large-scale sculpture seriously — even though the calculations later turned out to be wrong.

To his classmates, Donald Evans' sensibility seemed romantic and European. He loved playing with language and symbols and multiple meanings. He began to use a pseudonym, Doke Emmons. As a child he had been fascinated by ghosts and spiritualism, and at college he began to write down his dreams. He believed in the collective unconscious and in reincarnation, and he wondered about his past lives. He read Gurdjieff, and he investigated Scientology and worked at his own spiritual self-improvement.

Devoting himself to his work, he hardly ever exercised except for yoga. He took photographs of himself and his friend Steve Mensch and neatly cut out the heads and transposed them to put his face over his friend's muscular torso. He worried about his receding hairline and told Phoebe McGuire that his prime was past.

In January 1969, he graduated from Cornell with a bachelor's degree in architecture, and again he went off to Europe for a few months. When he came back to the United States, he moved to New York and joined Richard Meier and Associates, Architects, as an architectural designer.

Richard Meier was just becoming well-known and his office was a very busy and exciting place to work. Donald Evans showed talent at the profession and he worked hard on several prize-winning projects: private houses, Westbeth Artists' Housing in Manhattan, the Monroe Developmental Center in Rochester, New York and Twin Parks Northeast Housing in the Bronx. Eventually he was given the responsibilities of a construction and project supervisor.

He lived on Livingston Street in Brooklyn Heights in an apartment that he had furnished sparely and beautifully with a few simple pieces of old wooden furniture collected on his small salary. He kept his books and records hidden in closets. On the walls he hung prints and posters by artist friends, and on the kitchen shelves he displayed his collection of canned and packaged foods chosen for their labels.

He only slept there. Either he worked late at the office or, if he finished early, he made his rounds, going to galleries and visiting one friend after another; late at night he went back across the river to Brooklyn. In his spare time, he designed a few sets for an Off-Off Broadway theater. As always he was very frugal, saving for travel, and he earned extra money by helping friends, especially William Katz: fixing up his loft, executing décors and costumes for the Louis Falco Dance Company, assembling the deluxe rubber stamp album called *Stamped Indelibly.* He loved New York and made the most of it.

At the same time, he said the pace of his life in New York drove him crazy, and he felt uncommitted to his profession. The questions were: where to go and what to do. In his unhappy indecision he considered architecture elsewhere, perhaps in the Middle East, or illustration and graphic design in New York. In the back of his mind, though, he still thought about becoming an artist.

He shyly began to show his childhood work to friends. They were enthusiastic. In 1969 William Katz showed the tiny "Encyclopedia Britannica, c. 1953," in his loft in one of the exhibitions in a wooden box called Tabernacle on the Bowery. The group show in the miniature gallery was called "Slim Pickin's" and Donald Evans made the catalogue listing the other miniature works by his friends Robert Indiana, Cletus Johnson, Gerald Laing, Marisol and John Willenbecher.

Donald Evans showed the World Wide Stamp Album to the graphic designer Barry Zaid, who decided to take it to the designer Milton Glaser in hopes that some of the childhood stamps would be reproduced in a new magazine called *Audience.* The magazine folded and nothing happened, but Donald Evans began to think that perhaps people would be interested in his stamps; maybe he could earn his living exploring the world he had invented as a child.

In the art world ideas of image and scale had changed. Watercolors on small paper rectangles and typewritten catalogues weren't as "weird" as he had once felt them to be. Always concerned with stamps and the mails, he had met Ray Johnson and joined the New York Correspondence School. This informal group of people sent cryptic letters back and forth to one another. Donald Evans passed the letters on in envelopes he carefully decorated with his favorite American stamps. And then in 1971 he began again to paint his own commemoratives, a very few that he gave to friends.

That year he worried constantly about what to do, about "the 'why' of art and the 'I give up' of finding love and happiness," as he wrote to his friend the illustrator Jerry Joyner. Another letter to Jerry Joyner was sealed with a stamp that Donald Evans painted from a photograph of the country cottage in Holland where his friend was living. The stamp was inscribed with the Dutch address: Achterdijk (Behind the Dike) near the village of Schalkwijk, as if the cottage were a country; in the corners of the stamp are both their initials. Jerry Joyner invited him to come to visit.

Donald Evans began to save every penny he could. He sold his huge collection of real stamps to his father. In January 1972, after the office Christmas bonus, he quit his job, lent his furniture to friends, and gave up his apartment. In early February he packed up his watercolors and a stack of paper prepared with perforations and flew off to Holland "in a dream," he wrote to William Katz: "I just left and the world is so different and I don't understand anything."

He did know what he wanted to do though, and after the pressures of New York the quiet days in the Dutch countryside were perfect for his work. His first stamp in Holland showed the view to the dike from the cottage, and he imagined it was issued by the principality of Achterdijk.

He had brought his camera and he photographed Jerry Joyner and three American friends, the cottage where they all lived and the rural neighborhood. From the prints he painted postage stamps with landscapes and their portraits as the reigning royalty: HRH Princess Gloria (Kaiser), HRH Prince Jerry with the royal begonias, HRH Prince Louie (Denolfo) at the carnival, Prince Dick (Crawford) as Michelangelo, and himself as Prince Doke in the cottage doorway.

For a month the friends stayed at the cottage, and to pass the time they read and cooked, played what they called Red Door Darts and drank Dutch gin; and Donald Evans made his stamps. Every day when the postman came along the dike to deliver the day's letters, the friends would invite him in for a cup of coffee, to talk and to practice their Dutch. He was reluctant until Donald Evans showed him his new stamps.

Holland seemed to Donald Evans a perfect place to be: he liked the small scale of the country; Dutch openness to new ideas coupled with hardheaded practicality; an ongoing tradition in painting of small-scale realism; the high Dutch skies and special light; a national hobby of stamp collecting; and the soft guttural language with all its fond diminutives.

He found portents too: an old postcard of a woman in black he felt he had known in a past Dutch life; his initials DE on many shops (for Douwe Egberts coffee); and the rainbows that often arched down into the fields outside the cottage.

In March he moved to Amsterdam where he stayed and helped fix up an old warehouse that belonged to his friend Larry Hager. He had a rubber stamp made that read Donald Evans Amsterdam 1972 and he used it to cancel some of the new stamps he was making.

In 1972 he made 561 stamps from twenty countries, his rate of production carefully recorded on graphs. Once again he began to use his work as a kind of journal in which to record and celebrate his world, his friends and everything that interested him. Equipped with the capacities and techniques of an adult, he had recovered his childhood.

He used friends' names for European countries, like Dutch Nadorp and Scandinavian Yteke, and he asked friends for words that would trigger his imagination to make stamps from faraway places, like Middle Eastern Adjudani. He invented Gnostis to issue stamps of mystical symbols and rainbows and comets, and Amis and Amants to issue stamps about friendship and love. He revived the kingdom of Caluda from his childhood work as the mother country of newly independent ex-

colonies like Amis and Amants and Katibo to express his own feelings of independence as an artist. And he invented countries simply in order to paint things he liked: Mangiare for Italian food and Sung-Ting for Chinese ceramics.

People liked his work. He thought of it as "underground," but an Amsterdam dealer, Bram Volkers, asked to keep a few pieces to show to collectors and soon offered him a one-man exhibition. For it Donald Evans made a postcard announcement with a stamp from the country of Asselijn (the name of the gallery). The prices of the stamps started at about five dollars each, and they could be bought individually or in sets; he also offered to make stamps on commission.

Although he was successful, he wasn't earning a living, so in December 1972 he returned to New York where he worked again in architects' offices. He later said he had learned discipline and attention to detail from architectural drawing, and perhaps a certain sense of building a composition with stamps as little blocks. He continued to make his stamps, including some on commission for the *New York Times* on subjects like the Cold War, the B-1 bomber and Watergate.

In the summer of 1973, he went back to Holland with enough money to live and worked toward a second show in Amsterdam, this time with the dealer Cora de Vries; it was a success. He wrote to William Katz, "It is so interesting to be so involved in my *own* work. Stirring up long dormant feelings and capabilities. I am enjoying myself plunging into this business, ups and downs."

His health at the time was very bad. He was always a hypochondriac, but now he had a serious case of chronic pneumonia that was finally diagnosed as the result of an extra lung. He was afraid he might die in the operation to remove it, and his thoughts of death became the inspiration for Lichaam and Geest (Body and Soul), the twin kingdoms he imagined had once been invaded by ferocious killer whales.

He underwent the operation in early 1974 and as soon as it was over, he was back to painting stamps again. He wrote to William Katz, "Time seems to reckon itself according to periods of concentration and/or pleasure with friends." He continued, with even greater precision, to integrate the details of his life into his stamps. The countries of his imaginary world became representations of life in the real world.

In the flea market he found an old picture of a cottage that was a collage of stamps. He liked its resemblance to his life: his stamps had become his world.

His life was a history of work and growing success. He had show after show with dealers in many different cities in Europe and America. Each time he showed he sold more and more work, both to private and public collections. Living frugally, he could give up architecture for his stamps; he could travel and collect a few things again, including books for his work. And he delighted in giving his work to friends.

He lived and worked in many places: apartments and lofts of friends and tiny rented rooms in attics and basements. The portability of his work was perfect; he could carry a show, unframed, under his arm.

He had a large collection of visual information, books and photographs from which to work. Since he traveled so much and never had a permanent place to live, he left books with friends in different cities so that he could work from their illustrations when he came to visit. He had books on windmills and mushrooms, flowers, fruits and vegetables, old ships and planes, birds and birds' eggs; illustrated travel books; stamp catalogues and books on stamps and postal history; works of Gertrude Stein. And he had a few sea shells, a set of dominos and a lot of library cards.

He told the *Paris Review* that he used photographs a lot. "The images don't necessarily come out looking like the photograph, but I, for example, could never paint a camel out of my head that looked like a camel. I just don't have that gift." He did, however, learn enough about some things so that he could make up his own versions. The windmills, for example, on page 131 are from a book but the later series on page 35 and page 109 (his last finished work) are all of his own design. He used his books on stamps to look up period details but he never copied them; he wanted to solve all the problems of design for himself.

He always worked with his one trusty brush (a number two Grumbacher) and the same box of watercolors, as well as pencils and pens and colored inks. He worked on paper that he prepared with his own perforations to make different shapes (squares, rectangles or triangles), and he handled the tiny papers with tweezers. When he finished painting, he might cancel the stamps with an appropriate postmark carved from a rubber eraser with an X-acto knife: to make them look more real, to disguise mistakes or "to establish a certain kind of distance from the work," he told the *Paris Review*.

His eyesight was very sharp (he never used a magnifying glass), and he was careful to destroy the stamps he felt didn't work. The ones he liked he might arrange on an envelope or postcard chosen from his collection, and sometimes he added a real postal sticker or one he drew himself. Then he arranged the piece — individual stamps, envelopes or postcards — in the plastic pockets of the black stock sheets he used to display his work. He liked them because they were real stamp collectors' sheets and because the black background disguised the typewritten periods that he used instead of punched holes to resemble perforations.

He always worked in series and in actual stamp size. At the beginning, he painted individual stamps and then experimented with their layout. Later he sketched series whole, including subjects, colors, denominations and layout, before he started to paint.

The Glenveagh sketch sheet on page 18 shows the genesis of an entire imaginary country and its stamps. In September 1976 he went to visit Henry McIlhenny at his castle, Glenveagh, on Lough Veagh in County Donegal in the north of Ireland. As usual, Donald Evans was working and he decided to make a new country, Glenveagh, to honor his host.

On the left side he sketched the view from the dovecote down the lake. It became the subject repeated on a series of a dozen stamps he dated 1956. He worked out the colors and their arrangement as well as the placement of the cancellation in the titled sketch of the envelope on which he intended to mount the pictorials. In the line of half-drawn numbers at the top of the sheet he worked out how the frame of each stamp would fit around the top of the number of its denomination.

Below them he designed the postmark he planned to carve for Glenveagh's post office and he made a note of a source book for future reference. Then he made a list of denominations, colors and subjects for another series that he later painted, titled "1968. Fruits and vegetables from the gardens at Glenveagh."

At the bottom of the sheet is a list of four possible subjects for a third series that eventually became the "1958. Pictorials" landscape views of Glenveagh, each like the sketch in the lower right-hand corner with a "royal" portrait of Henry McIlhenny in profile in an oval frame.

He had early on solved the problem of titling his work by following the example of stamp catalogues. He named his stamps like real stamps, and included an issue date for each one. He kept a methodical record of everything he made, and this record became an integral part of his work: he called it the Catalogue of the World.

He organized the catalogue alphabetically by country, and within each country he arranged the stamps chronologically by the fictional date of issue. Achterdijk, for example, issued a series of windmills in 1958 that are illustrated on page 35. On the page from the catalogue on page 20 is a representative

GLENVEAGH

GLENVEAGH
FROM THE DOVECOTE

GLENVEAGH
FROM THE DOVECOTE

GLENVEAGH

GLENVEAGH
COUNTY DONEGAL
3
SEPT
76

GARDEN BULBS IN COLOR
McFarland
Hatton
Foley
McFarland / Macmillan
NY 1938

Lough veagh from The Dovecote
5 IX 76

① Approaching Glenveagh.
② The Castle
③ The Pleasure Garden
④ Lough Veagh
    Muckish Mountain

GLENVEAGH
MUCKISH MOUNTAIN

GLENVEAGH
COUNTY

stamp Xeroxed from the series and in this case hand-colored. The code in parentheses after the title tells where and when Donald Evans made the stamps: A for Amsterdam, XI. 1975 for November, 1975. Each of these stamps is signed and dated with his initials and the year he made it (sd: DE. 75). For this series he used watermarked Strathmore Script paper (SS), and the perforations he made with the periods on the particular typewriter number 7½ every two centimeters, according to the standard philatelic perforation gauge. He made these stamps on paper that he tinted with watercolor wash.

Then he listed the design found on each denomination, in this case his name for each windmill, and next the colors he used to paint them. The currency of Achterdijk is one hundred cents to one florin. The one florin stamp also exists outside the series in a variation with more perforations, in this case a print instead of a watercolor. He chose it to use on a poster for a show at the Vick Gallery in Philadelphia in 1976.

The paragraph after the list of colors tells the history of the piece's exhibition. The P indicates that he first showed these windmills in Paris at the Galerie Germain in December 1975 and then with his dealers in Rotterdam, Philadelphia and Washington, D.C., before they were sold (indicated by the colon) to a private collector in New York. The windmills have not been published before, but when a piece appeared in a book, catalogue or magazine, Donald Evans listed where and when it was reproduced.

Finally, at the bottom of the page, he recorded each time he had revised or added to the catalogue page itself, dating it as part of his work.

He wrote the catalogue in three languages: in English for exhibitions in England and the United States; in French as the Catalogue du Monde for Paris; and in Dutch as the Catalogus der Wereld for Holland. He also made one special edition of the stamps of Yteke for his friend Yteke Waterbolk.

Donald Evans made fifteen editions of his catalogue. At first, when he still sold individual stamps, he used it as a price list for collectors. Later, when he decided to sell only sets of stamps, he also offered Xeroxed copies of the catalogue for sale as works in themselves.

The catalogue grew to fill 330 pages. He revised and updated it with his new work and new information about his old work for each exhibition. Then he Xeroxed a few examples for presents to friends and for the gallery to have on hand. He limited the edition theoretically to the number of copies equal to his age, although he never made or sold that many. Each copy had a bonus: one Xeroxed stamp was hand-colored.

While he painted his stamps and listed the information about them in his catalogue, Donald Evans fantasized stories about his imaginary countries. He told the *Paris Review* a few of them, and he talked with his friend Remy Charlip, the writer, dancer and choreographer, about making a book with stamps and stories, a children's book to be called *Postcards to Gopshe*. Gopshe was Remy Charlip's dog, a Lhasa apso, and Remy Charlip had in fact sent the dog postcards when he was traveling. They decided to combine their fantasies and make an album of old postcards sent to Gopshe by Princess Yteke from her trip around the world in 1928. Whenever she saw something that reminded her of her Lhasa apso (flowers, trees, haystacks, waterfalls), she sent a card with a picture of it to her pet at home in the palace in Geest (Soul).

Donald Evans planned Princess Yteke's itinerary through the countries of his world and made travel notes about the places in order to guide Remy Charlip in writing the messages. He also designed the album and its layout and drew a map of his world for its endpapers. His stamps, of course, were to be mounted on the postcards.

The book was never finished. Donald Evans later told the *Paris Review* he himself hesitated to write down the stories of his countries in detail because he wanted his work to be open-ended. He wanted to leave room for the fantasies of his audience and for the expansion of his countries in his own imagination as he worked.

Donald Evans also thought very carefully about his shows, and he often made special pieces for them like the minarets of Adjudani on page 41 and the windmills of Sabot on page 131. He planned his exhibitions in lists to make sure to present as many varieties of work as he could, and he diagrammed the hanging of each show on his own floor plan of the particular gallery to give each piece the best context.

He saw to every detail himself: the framing of the pieces in the plastic box frames he had chosen; the design, printing and mailing of postcard announcements and posters. He photographed each piece and each gallery installation. He scaled his prices (eventually they ranged from $600 for a piece with ten or fewer stamps to $1,000 for a piece with more than twenty), and he arranged for newspaper and magazine articles, publicity and interviews.

During the course of an exhibition he spent as much time as he could in the gallery so that he could talk with visitors and personally show them his work. It was the only time he wasn't painting. For his last show at the Fischbach Gallery in New York, he put his brush and box of watercolors on display,

60c

1958. Windmills (A:XI.1975;sd:DE.75)
SS.Perf 7½; tinted paper
Designs: 1c.Achterdijk, 2c.Glorië, 3c.Vosburg, 4c.Prince Dick,
5c.Hager, 6c.Jan van Campen, 7c.Schalkwijk, 8c.Augustine,
9c.Lindaburg, 10c.Desiree, 11c.Joep, 12c.Prince Jerry,
15c.Dokesburg, 20c.Hanneke, 30c.Petersburg, 40c.Lodewijk,
50c.Claartje, 60c.Anneke, 80c.Femke, 1f.Achterdijk

```
 1c  ultramarine and black
 2c  dark lake and black
 3c  olive green and black
 4c  ochre and black
 5c  gray and black
 6c  green and black
 7c  orange and gray-black
 8c  violet and gray-black
 9c  orange-red and black
10c  ultramarine and black
11c  brown and gray-black
12c  carmine and black
15c  yellow and black
20c  pale green and gray-black
30c  lake and black
40c  violet and black
50c  olive green and gray-black
60c  orange-red and gray-black
80c  brown and gray-black
 1f  black and gray-black
     a. perf 11:printed in offset and issued as single stamp
```

P(XII.1975); Galerie Fenna de Vries, Rotterdam(II.1976);
Vick Gallery, Philadelphia(III-IV.1976); Fendrick Gallery,
Washington(IV-V.1976):Private collection, New York

20.XI.75, 26.XI.75, 4.II.76, 1.III.76, 2.VIII.76, 11.II.77

locked up in a glass case, just to make sure he would spend time talking and working with people at the gallery instead of painting more stamps.

His work was always improving technically. He told the *Paris Review:* "The more I do, the more crazy and minuscule the detail becomes and the more stamplike they become. And that intrigues me....One of the things I get excited about in making this work is that I try to make it look real."

At the same time, his visual record of the world became fuller and fuller. He painted an enormous variety of plants and animals, people and landscapes, from forty-two countries that range around the world from American My Bonnie to Chinese Sung-Ting. He made at least one issue for practically every year from 1852 to 1973. And he worked through what he called the permutations, all the possibilities of form and composition he could think of for a stamp and its presentation. He experimented with language, color, shape, repetition, variation, representation and abstraction. But underlying this complexity, the guiding principle for his work, he said, was: "basically that it describes something which I think is interesting and that it looks like a stamp."

Before he died at the age of thirty-one in a fire in Amsterdam, Donald Evans had painted and catalogued almost four thousand stamps. He said simply, "Stamps are terrifically rich."

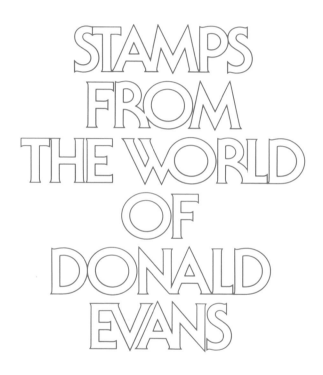

Donald Evans addressed this antique envelope to De Heer Naaktgeboren, Mr. Naked-born in Dutch. De Heer Naaktgeboren was one of Donald Evans' imaginary correspondents and a surrogate name he used for himself.

Donald Evans moved to Holland in 1972 to start a new life, and the stamps show the view from the first house he lived in there. One of the first Dutch words he learned was his address, Achterdijk (Behind the Dike) and he decided to use it in the new work he was making. Achterdijk became the name of both the country and its capital.

This monochromatic series of *postzegels,* or postage stamps, is dated 1852, the first issue of both Holland and Achterdijk. They are in values from one cent to five cents and imperforate, as stamps were before the introduction of the perforating machine to Holland in 1864. They had to be snipped apart with scissors; if the postage for a letter came to half a cent, a one cent stamp was cut in two. Donald Evans carved rubber erasers to make rubber stamps in target and grid patterns to resemble actual early cancellation markings.

This landscape is the view to the dike from his country cottage, across the flat green fields outlined with drainage ditches, to the distant line of poplars by a canal; above it all is the vast Dutch sky. This view was the subject of the first stamp Donald Evans painted in Holland and he repeated it again and again; this version of the view is the first work listed in his Catalogue of the World. Other times he painted it with a promising rainbow arching down toward the field, or with an airplane in the sky, as on the ninety cent stamp in the 1940 series.

Donald Evans was fond of triangular stamps and made many of them; in the two triangular series here he showed in period colors the development of Achterdijk's airmail with the introduction of puddle-jumper planes and silent zeppelins in serial motion, floating in overhead, and away again.

1852. Achterdijk landscape. (1974)

1940. Airpost. (1974)

1932. Airpost. Rate increases. (1974)

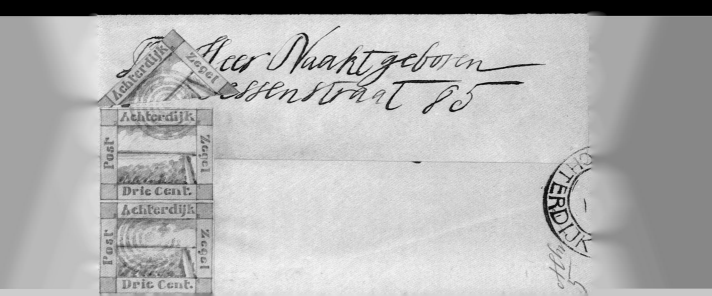

Every year in Holland, after the gray, damp winter, the Dutch post office celebrates the arrival of the long, bright days of the short summer with special summer stamps. Donald Evans made his summer stamps of Achterdijk as a model to show to the design committee of the Dutch post office for a possible commission.

The three ten cent stamps show a typical Dutch landscape similar to the view from the cottage at Achterdijk on page 25: through flat green fields a country road bordered by ditches stretches to a line of poplars; the seventeenth-century bell tower of an old brick and stone town and the sails of a windmill punctuate the flat green horizon line that meets the high blue sky.

Donald Evans was fond of the changing views he saw from the windows of Dutch trains, and he knew the old Dutch game of panoramic landscapes divided into cards to be set out and rearranged for various views. He designed this series, his most complicated panorama, so that it could be shuffled to make six variations on the still and even sameness of the countryside. Then he mounted his favorite arrangement on an unaddressed envelope.

1969. Panoramic Achterdijk landscape. (1976)

Donald Evans was fascinated by chickens. When he was a child in New Jersey, there were many poultry farms full of white leghorns, but he liked the more colorful and exotic breeds, especially the Bremen Spangle. He made a record on his stamps of what he learned about the birds. In this Achterdijk poultry series there are likenesses of twenty different breeds of *hoenders,* or chickens, with their Dutch names.

Gallus gallus was known long ago in southern Asia and the fighting cock on the *drie* (three) cent value resembles its aboriginal ancestors: tough, scrawny and long-legged, admired for its fighting spirit. Most chickens, though, have been bred for more domestic qualities, like meaty breasts and day-in, day-out egg laying. The British Dorking on the *vijftig* (fifty) was bred for its meat; the Mediterranean Leghorn (on the florin), Andalusian (on the *zestig,* or sixty) and Ancona (on the *twee,* or two) are prized for their egg production. In the last century newer general purpose breeds good for both meat and eggs were developed: the Dutch Barnevelder (on the *vier,* or four) and the American Plymouth Rock (on the *veertig,* or forty), the Wyandotte (on the *elf,* or eleven), and the Rhode Island Red (a brown-egg layer, on the *dertig,* or thirty).

After he learned the chickens' names and shapes and colors, Donald Evans planned the layout of a page of stamps in lists and sketches. Trying to organize a rhythm, he switched the elements around; here, for example, he settled on vertical end rows of chickens facing right and, for the leader, he chose the Spanish Whitecheek (on the *een,* or one) looking over its shoulder down the row.

The Betuwe is the rich orchard land of Holland just upriver from the cottage at Achterdijk. Donald Evans once painted a view of it in the triangular seventy cent airmail stamp on page 26. When he found a stack of old postcards with reproductions of paintings of varieties of apples and pears, he painted stamps to go with them from the imaginary orchards of Achterdijk.

In the series of pears there are ten cards and stamps in values from five cents to one florin and twenty-five cents; each stamp was painted from the card it is on, like a child's matching picture game. On this fifteen cent stamp and its card, which was Donald Evans' favorite of the group, is a Zwijn-drechtse *wijnpeer,* a wine-pear named for a Dutch town on the Maas River near Dordrecht.

By the time Donald Evans painted it he had decided to stay and work in Holland, and he had moved from the country into the city of Amsterdam. To celebrate his new home he ordered a new rubber postmark stamp that read: Donald Evans Amsterdam 1972. He put this imprint on his work and study books and he also used it to cancel this stamp.

1966. Pear of Achterdijk. (1972)

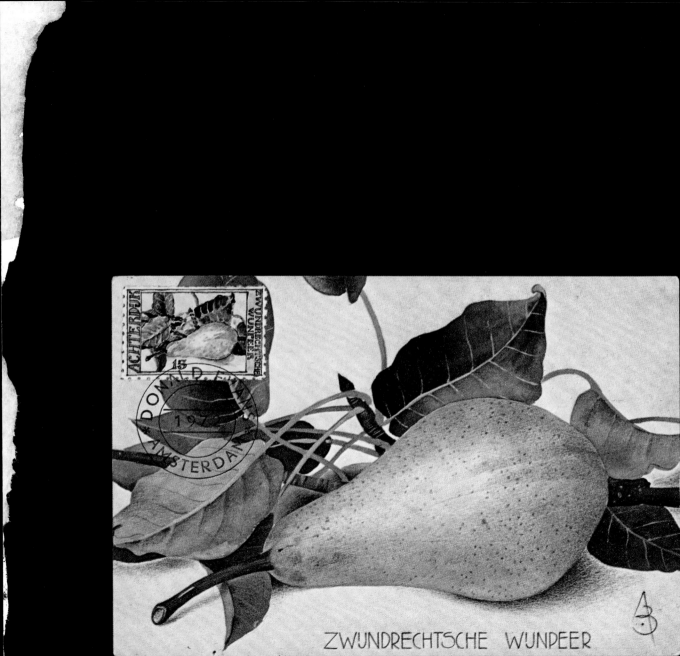

ZWIJNDRECHTSCHE WIJNPEER

To Donald Evans, Achterdijk seemed a good metaphor for the Netherlands, the low countries, which lie below the level of the sea. The cottage at Achterdijk was in the middle of the rich delta country the Dutch call "between the rivers," where the Rhine River fans out into several branches on its way to the North Sea. Like much of the Netherlands, without the windmills this area would still be a vast swamp or shallow lake.

The giant machines were used for centuries to harness the power of the wind that blows freely over the flat land to pump the water up and out. Although the windmills are now obsolete, the Dutch have preserved many of them in working order. Sails spinning, they dot the countryside and mark the outskirts of towns, a national symbol of ingenuity and hard work.

Donald Evans studied the architecture of the various kinds of windmills and then designed his own: a *wip* — or hollow wooden post — mill is found on the *elf* (eleven) cent stamp; an octagonal thatch-covered smock mill is on the *vijftig* (fifty) cent; a brick tower mill with a wooden stage on the *drie* (three). And as he painted them, he thought of them as abstract "portraits" and named them, as the Dutch do, after friends, such as Desirée and Joep. He named the Prince Jerry for his friend Jerry Joyner who had lived in the cottage at Achterdijk. Dokesburg — Doke's Town — on the *vijftien* (fifteen), is from Donald Evans' own nickname, Doke. Two he named after his country Achterdijk, the one cent and the one florin, where he painted a church tower in the distance.

 ACHTERDIJK — *Achterdijk* — **EEN**

 ACHTERDIJK — *Glorië* — **TWEE**

 ACHTERDIJK — *Vosburg* — **DRIE**

 ACHTERDIJK — *Prins Dick* — **VIER**

 ACHTERDIJK — *Hager* — **VIJF**

 ACHTERDIJK — *Jan van Campen* — **ZES**

 ACHTERDIJK — *Schalkwijk* — **ZEVEN**

 ACHTERDIJK — *Augustine* — **ACHT**

 ACHTERDIJK — *Lindaburg* — **NEGEN**

 ACHTERDIJK — *Desirée* — **TIEN**

 ACHTERDIJK — *Joep* — **ELF**

 ACHTERDIJK — *Prins Jerry* — **TWAALF**

 ACHTERDIJK — *Dukesburg* — **VIJFTIEN**

 ACHTERDIJK — *Hanneke* — **TWINTIG**

 ACHTERDIJK — *Petersburg* — **DERTIG**

 ACHTERDIJK — *Lodewijk* — **VEERTIG**

 ACHTERDIJK — *Claartje* — **VIJFTIG**

 ACHTERDIJK — *Anneke* — **ZESTIG**

 ACHTERDIJK — *Femke* — **TACHTIG**

 ACHTERDIJK — *Achterdijk* — **FLORIJN**

Donald Evans often asked friends for words that would trigger him to make stamps; one Dutch friend gave him Adjudani with the explanation that the word meant Jewish in Persian and was his father's Persian name. Donald Evans thought it was terrifically exotic. He transliterated it into French for the name of the country's post office, Postes Adjudanes, because he imagined French was the international diplomatic language the government used. But he didn't know Persian or Arabic, so when he noticed that his friend's backhand signature of his surname (Buis) looked vaguely Arabic, he decided to use it as the inscription on each stamp.

Adjudani's first issue in Donald Evans' catalogue is the ciphers from one to ten (reading left to right) whose shapes he learned.

An image on an old postcard suggested to him a native girl. He had painted a series with the pastel silhouette of a veiled woman in an ellipse on imperforate tinted rectangles that he imagined were another early issue, and he decided to surround the seductive girl with the images of the woman in purdah to whom, anonymous in her robes, he gave the name Queen Deliev, veiled spelled backward. The arrangement he chose is reminiscent of the way he played with stamps on the Domino express covers on page 70.

On the unaddressed envelope, he showed Adjudani natives wearing turbans. In order by value, they are: a southern turban, a townsman's fez, a round turban and a woman's turban.

1918. Ciphers. (1974)

1926. Veiled Adjudani woman. (1976)

1944. Turbans. (1974)

As a child, Donald Evans invented Middle Eastern countries in his imaginary world; sultanates and emirates with names like Aluala and Alamabu issued stamps that had mosques and men in fezzes on them. Adjudani was the successor to these countries, and for its stamps Donald Evans studied Middle Eastern architecture, especially minarets. He used them as Adjudani's architectural symbol as he had used the windmills for Achterdijk and his other Netherlandish countries.

In the Islamic world, minarets are built for the muezzins' calls to prayer; nowadays these are often broadcast with loudspeakers from the minarets' high galleries. For his first New York show, Donald Evans painted a series of minarets of twenty different Middle Eastern mosques, five of them in the capital Trebor (Robert spelled backward), named after King Trebor, the disguised name of his friend Robert Buis. (The coin of Nadorp is a Buis.) The stamps are in values of millièmes, or thousandths in French, of a dinar.

The names he gave them in his catalogue are: ½ millième, Kalal; 1m., Jami; 2m., Dnebra; 3m., Trebor; 4m., Trebor; 5m., Ghuta; 8m., Trebor; 10m., Trub (Burt spelled backward); 12m., Naram; 15m., Aladar (the first name of his New York dealer, Aladar Marberger — his minaret has strings of lights on it); 20m., Talra; 25m., Elet; 30m., Trebor; 35m., Zawija; 40m., Edar; 50m., Nabil (a friend whom he also named crown prince of Adjudani); 60m., Mashad; 75m., Trebor; 100m., Prodan (his friend Philip Nadorp's last name backward); 1 dinar, Debora (a friend whom he also crowned as a princess of Nadorp).

1952. Minarets. (1975)

Post offices often issue stamps that illustrate the means of transportation used to move the mails. Donald Evans followed that example with boats on seapost stamps and airplanes and zeppelins on airmail stamps. He liked to use birds too, including pigeons carrying letters for the pigeon post. For the only airmail issue of Adjudani he painted a series of a falcon in flight.

On a wall in his attic room in Amsterdam he had a plate of photographs, from Eadweard Muybridge's book *Animals in Locomotion,* of an ass kicking up its hind legs. Donald Evans took from it the idea of showing motion in his stamps, as if each stamp were one of a series of stop-action photographs, or stills from a movie. (The zeppelins on page 27 are a later and more elaborate development of the idea.)

Donald Evans particularly liked to study the movements of birds on the wing; here he showed the characteristic fast wing beat of a falcon in "slow motion." Adjudani issued the series because of the association of the ancient royal sport of falconry with Middle Eastern sheiks, who learned to breed the birds and trained them to hunt. The high-soaring falcon dives and kills its prey on impact.

1959. Airpost. Falcon in flight. (1974)

Donald Evans never set foot in Asia, but he loved to read about the Middle East, especially in British travel books. In his imagination Adjudani stretched from Turkey to Tibet across an enormous, varied landscape: coast and desert, marsh and mountain. He even annexed Tibet as Adjudani's Mountain Provinces in 1939.

He painted several series of views that show Adjudani's landscape and way of life, its monuments and means of transportation — all set in a special Levantine frame. Donald Evans dated these monochromes, Adjudani's first pictorials, 1929. They include real views of Iraq and Afghanistan, and he titled them in his catalogue: 1 millième (in the center of the top row), mountain valley; 2m., minaret; 3m. (the second row), spear fishing; 4m., dhow; 5m., palms in a storm; 10m., poling through the marsh; 12m., desert landscape; 20m., minarets of Trebor; 25m., wheat field; 30m., citadel; 50m., camel caravan.

Donald Evans painted the stamps of the 1938 issue in two colors and on them he included ruins for the first time: 1 millième, ancient tomb; 2m., citadel; 3m., walls of Trebor; 5m., dhows; 7m. (the first in the third row), marshlands; 8m. (the first in the second row), coastal olive groves; 10m., view to the sea; 12m., oasis; 15m., ancient viaduct; 20m., field of favas.

Donald Evans imagined that by the 1960's Adjudani was promoting tourist trade. The most recent issues have full-color views like these of the beautiful, unchanged countryside: 5 millième, fortress of Debora; 10m., citadel near Trebor; 15m., fishing boat; 20m., Royal Valley; 25m., desert; 30m., balancing rock; 35m., terraces; 50m., cavalier; 70m., beach; 100m., citadel of Prodan.

1929. Pictorials. (1974, 1975)

1938. Pictorials. (1974)

1964. Pictorials. Tourism promotion. (1974)

  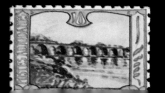 

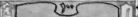

When Donald Evans began to make his stamps in Holland in 1972, he asked friends for names for new countries and looked to his childhood stamps for others. From his childhood World Wide Stamp Album he took his own imaginary Royaume de Calude, the Kingdom of Caluda in French, which he revived as the European mother country of four new colonies: Amis and Amants, the Azori Islands, the Islands of the Deaf and Katibo.

Amis and Amants means Friends and Lovers in French; Donald Evans loved the alliteration of the name. He imagined it as a tropical archipelago of idyllic islands populated with happy, friendly blacks (and later some Polynesians). This series of portrait heads of native islanders set in oval frames he inscribed with the initials RC for Royaume de Calude, which he imagined still ruled them at the time of this first issue.

He listed his subjects in his catalogue: 1 franc, Amant youth; 2f., Ami; 3f., woman of St. Rémy; 4f., Ami from St. Philippe; 5f., girl from Grand Amour; 8f., Ami; 10f., woman of St. Rémy; 12f., tribal chief; 15f., Ami; 20f., Bonne Amie; 25f., woman of St. Philippe; 50f., Amants' island chief.

1927. Colony of Caluda. Native islanders. (1974)

The many landscapes on the stamps of Amis and Amants are named, in French, for a condition of love or friendship. Donald Evans was always falling head over heels in love and believed in love at first sight, which the French call *coup de foudre,* literally thunderbolt. On these dozen stamps, the clouds are low and thick in the sky, threatening stormy weather. The combinations of colors suggest the different ways love strikes.

The stamps on the envelope show four islands in the long archipelago of love stretching from the little Premiers Amours (Puppy Love) toward distant L'Amour Perdu (Lost Love). Between them lie Ami des Beaux Jours (Fair Weather Friend) and Main-dans-la-Main (Hand in Hand). These four stamps are the first issue of the islands' autonomous administration, commemorating their first step toward independence from Caluda. Donald Evans canceled the stamps with the postmark of the islands' imaginary capital town, St. Philippe, dated 28 August 1945, his own birthday.

For the eight landscapes, he chose more French words. Céladon means Sentimental Lover. A Chaud Lapin, literally Hot Rabbit, is a Don Juan. Elan de Tendresse means Outburst of Tenderness. Coque-luche means Ladies' Man. La Passade means The Short Stay, literally, and figuratively, a passing fancy or brief intimacy. Les Propices means The Conciliations. Marivaudage is Witty Conversation (between lovers). Idolâtrie is Idolatry or doting.

1946. Coups de Foudre. Type of 1945. (1974)

1945. Autonomous administration. Island landscapes. (1974)

1955. Island landscapes. (1974)

AMIS ET AMANTS

·CELADON·

½

AMIS ET AMANTS

·CHAUD LAPIN·

1

AMIS ET AMANTS

·ELAN DE TENDRESSE·

2

AMIS ET AMANTS

·COQUELUCHE·

3

AMIS ET AMANTS

·LA PASSADE·

4

AMIS ET AMANTS

·LES PROPICES·

5

AMIS ET AMANTS

·MARIVAUDAGE·

6

AMIS ET AMANTS

·IDOLATRIE·

7

Donald Evans was fascinated by weaving. At   college he had learned how to dye wool yarn with natural dyes and weave it into cloth.   For friends he made long winter scarves dyed red with cochineal; he also made an   enormous one-piece fringed blanket three yards by two yards. For that he chose the pattern of the bright red and green tartan of the MacQuarrie clan in honor of his friend Phoebe McGuire and her family (McGuire is another form of the old clan name MacQuarrie).

The McGuires shared with Donald Evans a love of antiques and the old clan tartans. When he decided to paint the checkered patterns on his stamps, he invented a new republic named Antiqua to honor them, with its capital at Newcastle, the name of the town in Maine where the McGuires live.

In his playful notes for a proposed book called *Postcards to Gopshe,* Donald Evans said Antiqua was a coastal country with a rough climate, and the pagan population was superstitious, clannish and conservative. He imagined the Antiquans were weavers.

This series is a sampler of eight of the twelve tartans he painted as the only subjects of the stamps of Antiqua. Each stamp shows a sett, the characteristic unit of a tartan's pattern which is set up and repeated on the loom. The brightly colored ones, like the MacLeod on the ten penny stamp and the MacMillan on the twenty, are called dress tartans; the more muted ones, like the Gray Douglas on the forty, are called hunting tartans, designed to be worn on the moors.

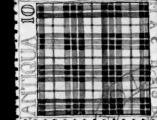

A "plaid" was a length of tartan cloth that a Highlander or Antiquan wore as kilt and cloak by day and slept under at night. It measured six yards by two yards, twice the length of the blanket Donald Evans made. To weave a plaid, the basic pattern of the sett is repeated over and over; Donald Evans decided to do that also in his stamps, with the variation of repeating the dark gray borders in each stamp's frame.

Over the rectangular stripes he painted the twill of the woven cloth, the parallel diagonal ribs that are made by weaving the weft threads over one and under two of the warp threads. In the margins of this perforated sheet he lettered the imprint of the imaginary printer and plate position numbers as well as a tiny DE 73, his dated signature.

The Gray Douglas was Donald Evans' favorite and he always kept this sheet of stamps framed on his wall in Amsterdam.

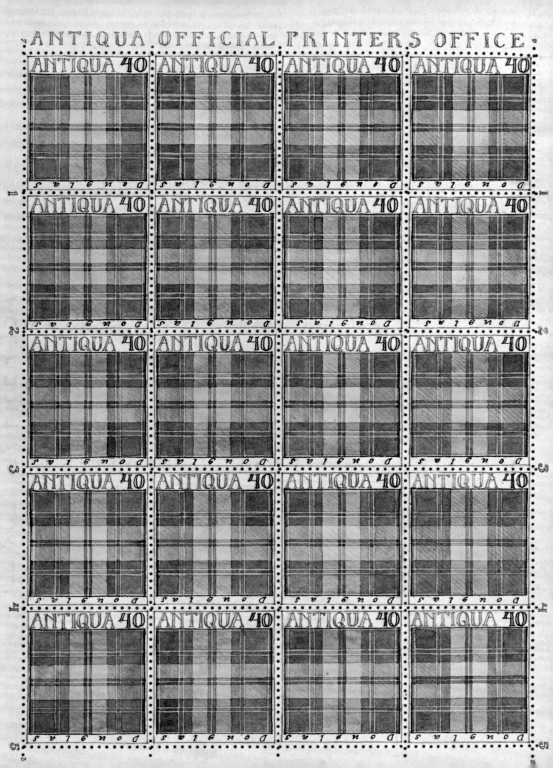

Banana

Bananagate was the newspapers' name for a political scandal in Honduras in early 1975. Donald Evans was delighted with the name and decided to make stamps for his own slightly corrupt Central American country, the Republica de Banana. This is the first issue he painted for his banana republic.

As in the children's game of matching cards, each of the cryptic national symbols appears twice (each time on the same-colored field but in a different-colored frame). They are a Bananian palm against sky blue, a shiny boot of the presidential guard, a shrimp from the Gulf, the crossed arrows of fraternity tied with a blue ribbon, a rose with thorns, a scorpion with its nippers and stinger, a flag swagged on its staff, an open umbrella, a pear and a ripe banana, the national symbol.

He used the Spanish standard of one hundred centavos to one peso for the currency and called the capital Chiquita, Little Girl in Spanish, after the United Fruit Company's cartoon character who used to appear on a round sticker on nearly every banana in Holland and America. He later invented the monuments of the city: the cathedral Santa Banana, the national palace, the plaza, the *avenida*, the Casino Banana d'Oro, as well as the national zeppelin La Banana Grande.

1960. Bananian symbols. (1975)

REPUBLICA DE BANANA CORREOS 1 CENTAVO

REPUBLICA DE BANANA CORREOS 2 CENTAVOS

REPUBLICA DE BANANA CORREOS 3 CENTAVOS

REPUBLICA DE BANANA CORREOS 4 CENTAVOS

REPUBLICA DE BANANA CORREOS 5 CENTAVOS

REPUBLICA DE BANANA CORREOS 6 CENTAVO

REPUBLICA DE BANANA CORREOS 7 CENTAVOS

REPUBLICA DE BANANA CORREOS 8 CENTAVOS

REPUBLICA DE BANANA CORREOS 9 CENTAVOS

REPUBLICA DE BANANA CORREOS 10 CENTAVOS

REPUBLICA DE BANANA CORREOS 15 CENTAVOS

REPUBLICA DE BANANA CORREOS 20 CENTAVOS

REPUBLICA DE BANANA CORREOS 30 CENTAVOS

REPUBLICA DE BANANA CORREOS 50 CENTAVOS

REPUBLICA DE BANANA CORREOS 75 CENTAVOS

REPUBLICA DE BANANA CORREOS 1 PESO

REPUBLICA DE BANANA CORREOS 2 PESOS

REPUBLICA DE BANANA CORREOS 3 PESOS

REPUBLICA DE BANANA CORREOS 5 PESOS

REPUBLICA DE BANANA CORREOS 10 PESOS

One of Donald Evans' favorite spots for a rendezvous in Amsterdam was a small bar near the Rijksmuseum that he commem- orated in the stamps of the country Barcentrum. After a day of painting and later prowling the town (the flea market, the shops, the galleries), he would stop to meet his friends in this cozy café with its warm yellow light and large, half-curtained windows, to talk of art and love.

It is an artists' haunt, and in the stamps of Barcentrum he celebrated the births and marriages, the children and families of his friends who were the royalty of the country.

This series shows what the natives drink in Bar-or-Table, the capital. Excellent Dutch coffee, thick and dark, for the sober. A *pilsje* (a small draft beer) at ninety cents to quench the thirst. One hundred cents equals one *Grotepils* (a large beer), the G of the currency, to sip as the afternoon wears on. Or for the same tariff, one of the famous genever gins, soft and smooth, young or old, sometimes flavored with berries or lemon, for a nip on the run. A chaser of orange juice, and on to a companionable glass of sherry as the daylight fades. In the evening after dinner, perhaps a local herb-flavored liqueur to aid the digestion, or a whisky or cognac. And then, why not? One for the road, a nightcap of whisky and soda. And so to bed. *Slaap lekker,* sleep tight.

1965. Drinks of Barcentrum. (1973)

BARCENTRUM
Koffie
0,50

BARCENTRUM
Pilsje
0,90

BARCENTRUM
Grotepils
1,00

BARCENTRUM
oude
1,00

BARCENTRUM
bessen
1,00

BARCENTRUM
citroen
1,00

BARCENTRUM
Jonge
1,00

BARCENTRUM
Jus d'Orange
1,25

BARCENTRUM
Sherry
1,50

BARCENTRUM
Binnenlands   Likeuren
1,75

BARCENTRUM
Whisky
2,50

BARCENTRUM
Cognac
3,00

BARCENTRUM
Long   Drinks
3,50

Cadaqués is a secluded fishing village north of Barcelona on the Costa Brava, the rugged coast of Catalonia. The white-washed town looks out on the Mediterranean from the steep hills that surround its harbor. Artists have summered there for years, and when Donald Evans went there in the summer of 1975, he stayed with the artist and critic Suzi Gablik in Marcel Duchamp's old apartment. There on the terrace he painted watercolor postcards of the view to send to friends and postage stamps from a new country called Cadaqués.

Every day he walked in the olive and almond groves that cover the hillsides, and swam in the sea. He roamed the markets and learned the Catalan words for the things he saw. He brought home fruits and vegetables as models for his stamps and after he painted them he cooked them. In Cadaqués he made one of his favorite dishes, stardust salad, a rice salad sprinkled with bits of sweet pepper cut painstakingly into little stars.

On these stamps he painted the sweet red pepper, parsley, lettuce, a zucchini, a pear, an eggplant, garlic, a mussel, a tomato, an olive, a peach, a cucumber and a lemon. Later he repeated the eggplant and the olive and painted stamps of the view of the harbor and the church. He mounted the four of them on an envelope, canceled them with a special postmark, and gave the piece to Suzi Gablik.

1960. Fruits and vegetables. (1975)

Donald Evans had several friends, some who were deaf and some able to hear, who could "sign." To communicate with them he learned the hand positions for finger-spelling the alphabet from a printed card that he carried with him. He also learned some hand-talk, the gestures that stand for words and phrases.

From this came the Islands of the Deaf, Iles des Sourds in French, a country where he imagined French was the official written language. It is a tropical archipelago, and was once a colony of the globe-circling Caludan empire. Since 1954 it has been an independent republic.

He called the capital Langue-des-Mains, or Hand-Talk, which he took from the title of a book by his friend Remy Charlip, and he located it on the island of Grand Sourd. *Honi soit qui mal y parle* is the national motto, shamed be he who speaks badly of it, which appears under the coat of arms, with a hand by an ear and a mouth. The standard of currency is one hundred centimes to one Pat, named for a deaf friend.

In this series, the third of three versions he made for the Islands of the Deaf, he showed the ciphers from one to ten in three ways: Arabic numerals, French words and the hand positions for the signs (including the arrows for the wagging hand that indicates the ten), on background colors that range in order through the spectrum. In his notes for *Postcards to Gopshe,* Donald Evans said there was a rainbow every day over the beautiful, silent archipelago.

1960. Ciphers. Type of 1959. (1975)

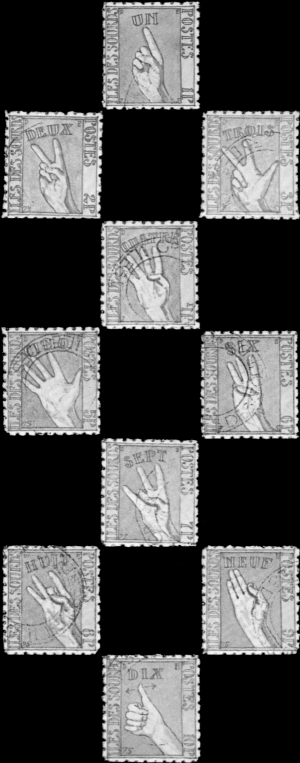

Donald Evans usually painted a complete image on each stamp he made, but for the Islands of the Deaf he made two sets about the geography of the archipelago in which the view is spread over several stamps. The first is a panorama of the islands, stretching from Grand Sourd to the Petits Sourds; the second, here, a close-up of the middle island.

In this block of four stamps, he celebrated the three-hundredth anniversary of the discovery of the Island Mountain of the Deaf by a seventeenth-century Caludan schooner, dwarfed in its shadows. The highest island in the chain, a snow-capped sugarloaf, it rises straight out of the sea and reaches up to the clouds, breaking out of Donald Evans' usual horizontal frame.

It is one of the several mysterious mountains that Donald Evans painted, and is reminiscent, except for the snow, of the Caribbean island of Saba. He in fact climbed that cloud-capped, extinct volcano in 1971 and painted many postcards of the view toward it from the beaches of the nearby island of St. Martin.

1965. Tercentenary of the Island Montagne-des-Sourds. Souvenir sheet. (1974)

In interviews, Donald Evans said he made domino stamps because he liked the game. He liked the sound of dominos and the way they look, so he invented a newly independent country called Domino and put them on its stamps.

In his notes for *Postcards to Gopshe,* he said the game of dominos is the national sport and industry of the former colony that supplies dominos to the world. He imagined a Domino museum with sets made of everything from mother of pearl to raisin bread.

Out of the twenty-eight pieces in a regular playing set, he eliminated the double blank and chose one piece for each stamp value from one to twelve, using the blank-ended and five-ended stones because he liked the composition of the dots.

When he had painted a series of twelve stamps, complete with rivets and cracks like those of his own antique ivory and ebony set, he began to think about playing a game with them. He positioned them around the edges of an envelope, matching the ends as they would be in an actual game. In the remaining empty space he put a French express sticker, upside-down to make it more abstract and harder to read, as an anchor to the composition. Then he canceled the stamps with the postmark he had carved for the Republic of Domino's post office in the capital of Boisivoires (Ivorywoods in French). Donald Evans often addressed Domino envelopes to his friends, and for their birthdays he put together their ages in the country's stamps.

For Domino, as for Antiqua, he also made full perforated sheets of stamps of a single value, such as the thirty-six two franc stamps printed, he imagined, by the Imprimerie Dominoise (the Domino Printing Office) for the Etat Domino (Domino State).

1932. Dominos. (1973)

1932. Dominos. (1974)

1938. Dominos. (1975)

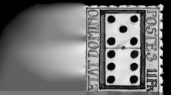

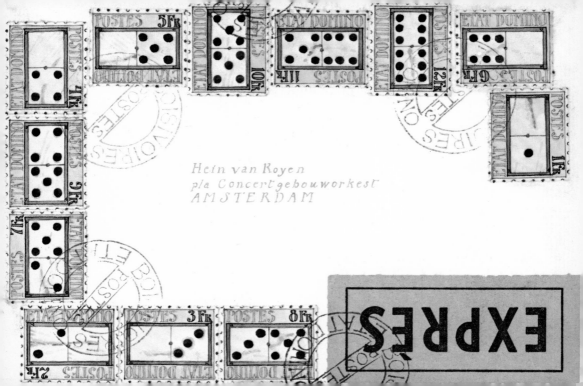

Hein van Royen
p/a Concertgebouworkest
AMSTERDAM

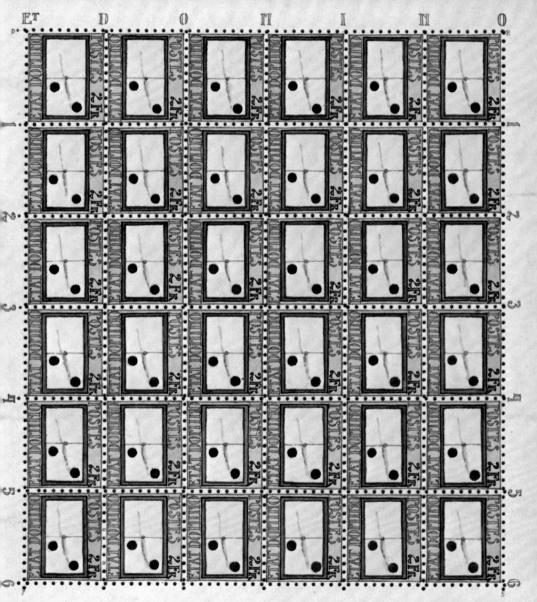

ET DOMINO

Imprimerie Dominoise 1938

Donald Evans' mythical kingdom of Fauna was the predecessor of the federal kingdom of Fauna and Flora. The kingdom's stamps are valued in the old pre-decimal English system, from a farthing to a pound. They all bear the image of a puffin in flight, reminiscent of the stamps of the little island of Lundy off the English coast that are prized by collectors of real stamps; since childhood Donald Evans had had a book about Lundy's postal history.

This full pane of imperforate halfpenny stamps is an example of a classic form of serious philately which collectors call plating. The collector reconstructs a sheet of stamps in the order they appeared on the original printing plate. Here the position of each stamp on the plate of thirty-six is marked in the oval gap midway in the frame, by letter for horizontal row and number for the vertical, A1 to F6.

Donald Evans worked to make each bird look the same and then varied the composition by cutting the stamps into different shapes, by singeing the edges of some of them on his stove to age them and by canceling them with different rubber stamps. He included his signature in the two overlapping stamps of the D and E rows.

Donald Evans' friend Remy Charlip had suggested to him a character named Professor Gluback, president of the Royal Philatelic Society of Yteke who, as Donald Evans' imaginary stamp collector, managed to reconstruct this pane of the rare carmine variation from many examples from many different sheets. A later Gluback reconstruction of the 144-stamp sheet of the lilac farthing was Donald Evans' largest work, and he called it his "most extravagantly crazy."

1868. Puffin in flight. (1976)

   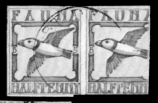

Fauna and Flora

On a trip to England in November and December of 1972, Donald Evans visited the Natural History Museum in London with his friend Jon Brunner. To celebrate the interest they shared in animals and plants, Donald Evans invented a new country called Fauna and Flora, a federal kingdom that had been united in 1925.

In his notes for *Postcards to Gopshe,* he said Fauna and Flora is an enormous country. The Isles of Flora have plants of every description. He named the capital Trillium after the wild flower that blooms in the spring and grows in the woods around a lake near his childhood home in New Jersey.

He painted these stamps of wild flowers from colored postcards published by the New York Botanical Garden. He put the first stamp he made in this series, the nine penny with the wood hyacinth, on the face of a postcard he once sent to his friend Phoebe McGuire for her birthday. Their common birth year, 1945, is the year of issue. He painted each flower twice, one to put on a card and one to include in this set of six.

Each of these is an American flower and, in order of value, their common names are: the Mexican gold poppy, the painted trillium, the wood hyacinth, the Indian pipe or trumpet pitcher plant, the bottle gentian, and the grass-leaved arrowhead. The Mexican poppy was his favorite.

1945. Wild flowers. (1973)

FAUNA & FLORA 3 *Eschscholtzia Flexiona*

FAUNA & FLORA 6 *Trillium Undulatum*

FAUNA & FLORA 9 *Penstemon Cobaea*

FAUNA & FLORA 1 *Sarracenia Alata*

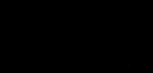

FAUNA & FLORA 13 *Gentiana Andrewsii*

FAUNA & FLORA 1/6 *Sagittaria Graminea*

Donald Evans often visited zoos and natural history museums to look at the animals, live and stuffed. He was particularly fond of penguins. When he was a child he made, among many stamps of different birds, a stamp from a vaguely English country he called Bournemouth. In an oval frame on this stamp was a portrait of the ruler Margaret Regina VIII; beside her waddled a flock of Gentoo penguins.

In an interview with the editors of the *Paris Review* in the spring of 1975, Donald Evans said he had wanted for some time to learn more about the different kinds of penguins, but hadn't yet found a book, partly out of laziness. When he did acquire one later that year, he painted this set in pale monochromes that suggest the habitat of these comically elegant, flightless birds (southern cousins of the flying puffin) whose wings have evolved into flippers, for swimming.

Donald Evans used fifteen different species which he placed in nichelike frames. On the farthing value, he filled out the set with a fluffy young chick of the emperor penguin, largest of them all. The emperor breeds on the ice in the Antarctic winter, and incubates its egg and cradles the chick balanced on top of its fleshy feet through months of darkness.

1938. Penguins. (1975)

Young Emperor

Jackass

Galapagos

Yellow-eyed

Rock-Hopper

White-Flippered

Magellan

Fairy
or Blue

Humboldt

Gentoo

Adélie

Crested

Chinstrap

Macaroni
or Royal

King

Emperor

Le dîner, o jantar (the dinner, in French and Portuguese, respectively) is the entry in Donald Evans' travelers' phrase book that he circled for the name of his Portuguese-speaking country, Jantar.

He had picked up the pocket dictionary in Paris and studied it before a holiday trip he took to Portugal, Madeira and the Canary Islands with his parents in December of 1973 and January of 1974. The dictionary was small, and lacked the words for many of the things he saw in the markets, so when he went to a café or restaurant he would order what he wanted by drawing pictures for the waiters. They taught him the Portuguese words which he then memorized and placed on the stamps of Jantar. The capital of Jantar he called Amesa (the table), and the standard of currency is one million réis to one conto (enough to buy a house in old Portuguese money).

Here are Donald Evans' English translations from the Portuguese as he listed them in his Catalogue of the World. The vegetables: ½ réis, avocado; lr., pea; 2r., watercress; 3r., carrot; 4r., turnip; 5r., parsley; 6r., lettuce; 7r., sweet pepper; 8r., onion; 9r., beetroot; 10r., cucumber; 11r., fennel; 12r., lentils; 15r., pumpkin; 20r., fava; 25r., garlic; 30r., tomato; 40r., olive; 50r., christophine; 100r., French beans; 200r., mushroom; 250r., cauliflower; 300r., walnut; 500r., rice; 1,000r., potato.

The seafood: 1 réis, oyster; 2r., limpet; 3r., mussel; 4r., clam; 5r., crab; 10r., squid; 20r., sea urchin; 50r., octopus; 100r., lobster.

And the short orders: 1 réis, *galão* (a large café au lait in a glass); 2r., muffins; 3r., black coffee; 4r., tea; 5r., sandwich; 10r., white coffee; 20r., toast; 50r., lemon round; 100r., beer.

1961. Vegetables. (1973-1974)

1958. Seafood. (1973-1974)

1960. Short orders. (1973)

 **MEIO** — a abacate

 **UM** — a ervilha
 DOIS — agriões
 TRES — a cenoura

 **QUATRO** — o nabo
CINCO — a salsa
SEIS — a alface
 SETE — a pimenta
 **OITO** — a cebola

 **NOVE** — a beterraba
DEZ — o pepino
 **ONZE** — o funcho
 **DOZE** — as lentilhas
QUINZE — a abóbora
 VINTE — a fava
 VINTE E CINCO — o alho

 **TRINTA** — o tomate
QUARENTA — a azeitona
 **CINQUENTA** — a pepinela
 **CEM** — os feijões
 **DUZENTOS** — o cogumelo

 **DUZENTOS CINQUENTA** — a couve-flor
 **TREZENTOS** — a noz
   **QUINHENTOS** — o arroz

 **MIL** — a batata

1 UM 1 · CORREIO · JANTAR · *a ostra*

2 DOIS 2 · CORREIO · JANTAR · *a lapa*

3 TRES 3 · CORREIO · JANTAR · *o mexilhão*

4 QUATRO 4 · CORREIO · JANTAR · *a amêijoa*

5 CINCO 5 · CORREIO · JANTAR · *o caranguejo*

10 DEZ 10 · CORREIO · JANTAR · *a lula*

20 VINTE 20 · CORREIO · JANTAR · *ourçinho do mar*

50 CINQUENTA 50 · CORREIO · JANTAR · *o polvo*

100 CEM 100 · CORREIO · JANTAR · *a lagosta*

Donald Evans imagined that his king-dom of Caluda had claimed a vast territory on the northern coast of South America, part of the Guianas, which was incorporated into the empire as the Etats d'Outremer (the Overseas States). On its early colonial stamps he painted happy natives similar to the ones in the series from Amis and Amants on page 49.

But in the later pictorials he showed a more realistic view of life in the colony. The subjects (taken from old photographs of South Carolina) are a fort in ruins, a woman staking her cow, a tidal inlet, a woman standing before her house and villagers returning from work. (The fishing boat is empty and the cow is bony.) Evidently the natives lead a downtrodden life of rural poverty, living in one-room wooden shacks, under the lovely palms perhaps, but not much has changed since the days of slavery. The postcard, on the other hand, shows the villas and gardens at Pointes Noires that belong to the rich white colonials who stand smiling in the road, holding their topees.

Symbolically, one of them is walking away toward the horizon, and a black woman carrying a bundle on her head is approaching. In 1940, Donald Evans imagined, there was a revolution; the Caludans left and the natives took over. A new black republic was formed called Katibo, and before they managed to print their own stamps, they simply overprinted the new name on the old colonial issues.

1940. Pictorial stamps of 1931 (Colonial administration) overprinted in black. (1974)

- POINTES NOIRES. — Maisons d'habitations Européennes

For Katibo's first issues, Donald Evans made four series of stamps which he dated each year from 1940 to 1943. Each series of nine stamps shows three uninhabited landscapes three times, typical views of the savannah, the beach and the islands, but they vary in color, lettering, perforation and value. The weather, simultaneous sun and showers, stays the same.

No longer in Caludan cents and francs, the values are in the new national currency, one hundred Luciens to one Riekje, which Donald Evans named after a Surinamese friend, Lucien Lafour, and his Dutch wife. (He worried that Lucien might take offense, but they both felt honored.) He carved the postmark with the name of the capital Par'bo, a brand of Surinamese beer and a contraction of Paramaribo, the country's capital. He dated the postmark 28 8 45, his birthday.

As he learned more about Surinam, he developed Katibo in other stamps. He extended the geography from the coastal strip, back up the black rivers into the jungles of the interior and up to the waterfalls of the southern mountains. He showed commercial crops — bananas, copra, cotton, lumber and rubber — being harvested and brought to market. And he showed the country's progress from the poverty of its early colonial days to economic development: a new shipyard and off-shore oil rigs, a new polyclinic and steel-and-glass high rises built along the Boulevard Lafour of the capital.

1941. Landscapes. Type of 1940 redrawn. (1974)

Katibo

Donald Evans' architect friend Lucien Lafour had suggested the word Katibo as the name for the republic; he told him it was Taki-Taki (Surinamese dialect) for a black man who sets himself free. Donald Evans painted portraits of *les Katiboises,* the women of proud young Katibo who had set themselves free.

He made three series of seven stamps each, painted from photographs he found on postcards and in books of Surinamese and African people. He listed these subjects, all blacks, in his catalogue as: a tribal woman, an official's wife from Par'bo, a tribal chieftess, a university student, a tribal woman, a patrician and a doctor. He imagined that the tribal women were Bush Negroes, the descendants of escaped slaves who still lead isolated lives in the Surinamese interior, following their ancestors' traditional African way of life. He represented the Westernized urban blacks with the student, the doctor from the new polyclinic and the stylish wife of the president.

He also painted special souvenir sheets of some of Katibo's women to celebrate the country's anniversaries of independence, with the patriotic inscription *Vive la République Katiboise.*

1957. Women of Katibo. (1975)

Donald Evans made this postcard piece as a birthday present for a friend in Holland. He imagined that the picture was of two young Katibois friends and on it he mounted second versions of three stamps from a series of women from Katibo.

In his portraits, he included people of the various ethnic groups that live in Surinam — Amerindians, East Indians, Hindus, Negroes and Creoles, with their varied facial types, hairdos and dress. The coat of arms he designed is half black and half white, suggesting racial harmony.

There is an East Indian woman on the one Lucien stamp, an official's wife is on the two and a tribal chieftess with elaborately knotted hair is on the five. The official's wife he took from a favorite photograph in a German travel book about a tour of Africa made between the wars; in the book the photograph of the woman was called *Asphaltblüte*, asphalt flower. He made three different stamps of her (in her white suit, Panama hat, earrings and black neck ribbon) because, he said, she was really the wife of the ruler (and an official herself) who liked to appear anonymously on the republic's stamps. Even Katibo was a little corrupt.

1962. Women of Katibo. (1976)

Lichaam and Geest is Dutch for Body and Soul. Donald Evans imagined that Body and Soul were twin kingdoms somewhere in northern Europe, independent until 1870 when they were united with several other Dutch-speaking territories as provinces of the new kingdom of Yteke.

Paintings of northern and arctic animals are shown on the kingdom's first two postal issues: the single 1853 *vijf* (five) ij stamp with a furry baby seal (reminiscent of an early issue of Newfoundland), and the seven 1855 stamps redesigned without spelled-out numbers. The animals are: an arctic fox, a beluga whale, a narwhal, a polar bear, the baby seal, a marten and a porcupine. The unit of currency Donald Evans named after the IJ, the harbor of Amsterdam, and *ijs,* ice in Dutch.

He stained the envelope to make it look like a postal rarity that philatelists call a disaster cover, a piece of mail that has survived a fire, wreck or other calamity and is eventually delivered. In this case, the addressee is De Heer Naaktgeboren (Mr. Naked-born), who has evidently moved since 1852 from Achterdijk to Geest, the capital city of the twin kingdoms.

Donald Evans made the envelope in a hospital bed in Amsterdam while recuperating from an operation to remove his third lung. He felt newborn, like his surrogate character's name, and sound in mind, like the envelope's address, Alhier bij Geest (literally, In the Neighborhood of Spirit).

1853. Baby seal. (1973)

1855. Animals. (1973, 1974)

In 1972 Donald Evans went to Italy. He was excited by Italian food and while in Rome he invented his Italianate country, Lo Stato di Mangiare (The State of Eating) and painted a block of four stamps, the Pesto Production Promotion, issued in the capital Basilicum. He liked basil and always had a pot of it growing in his attic room in Amsterdam.

Donald Evans had taught himself to cook from books, and his favorite cookbook writer was Elizabeth David. He particularly loved her versions of two herb-based sauces, messine and pesto, and he made stamps for them both.

He had painted stamps for sauce messine in 1971 to commemorate a dinner he cooked in his Brooklyn apartment for his friend Cletus Johnson. On those stamps a view of the Brooklyn Bridge is surrounded with the ingredients for the meal including chervil, parsley and tarragon for the sauce and a chicken to go under it; the inscription is Postes Messines.

Donald Evans based the pesto stamps of Mangiare on European recipe postcards that show the basic ingredients of a particular dish. The block of stamps, inscribed *Per fare il pesto*, to make pesto, shows the essentials of the sauce: a stalk of large-leafed sweet basil, pine nuts, a head of garlic cloves and a little wheel of strong Sardo cheese beside a hand grater; in the corner of each stamp he put a sprig of olive leaves with some fresh olives to symbolize the virgin oil that binds the other ingredients together after they have been pounded by hand in a mortar and pestle.

1968. Pesto Production Promotion. (1972)

Mangiare

On one Italian trip Donald Evans painted a series of twenty-five fruits and vegetables whose Italian names he had learned, just as he later learned Portuguese and painted the stamps of Jantar. When he returned to Italy again in the early summer of 1974, he stayed in Florence with his friend Erik Roos and painted a second series of thirty fruits and vegetables. He worked from fresh produce he bought in the markets and from an illustrated Italian book *I Frutti della Terra* (which he also used for most of the vegetables of Nadorp on pages 110 and 111).

He started with the pale green pea stamp and worked up to the watermelon, including along the way an edible squash blossom, a truffle, and a few herbs and nuts. For the higher values he set off his subjects with a contrasting color for the background and frame. Mangiare's currency is in Italian market weights: one hundred g. (for grams) to one e. (for etto, a hectogram, about 3½ ounces) and ten etti to one k. (for kilogram).

The English translations from Donald Evans' Italian shopping list, as he entered them in his catalogue, are: ½ gram, pea; 1g., apricot; 2g., zucchini blossom; 3g., sweet pepper; 4g., truffle; 5g., rosemary; 6g., prickly pear; 7g., almond; 8g., orange; 9g., asparagus; 10g., potato; 11g., peach; 12g., olive; 15g., loquat; 20g., grape; 25g., caper; 30g., blackberry; 40g., plum; 50g., cabbage; 60g., bay leaf; 75g., strawberry; 80g., celery; 1 etto, broccoli; 1¼e., pine nut; 1½e., cherry; 2e., radish; 2½e., persimmon; 3e., quince; 5e., spinach; 1 kilogram, watermelon.

1934. Fruits and vegetables. (1974)

LO STATO DI MANGIARE
½ PISELLO ½

LO STATO DI MANGIARE
1 ALBICOCCA 1

LO STATO DI MANGIARE
2 FIORE DI ZUCCHINO 2

LO STATO DI MANGIARE
3 PEPERONE 3

LO STATO DI MANGIARE
4 TARTUFO 4

LO STATO DI MANGIARE
5 ROSMARINO 5

LO STATO DI MANGIARE
6 FICO D'INDIA 6

LO STATO DI MANGIARE
7 MANDORLA 7

LO STATO DI MANGIARE
8 ARANCIA 8

LO STATO DI MANGIARE
9 ASPARAGI 9

LO STATO DI MANGIARE
10 PATATA 10

LO STATO DI MANGIARE
11 PESCA 11

LO STATO DI MANGIARE
12 OLIVA 12

LO STATO DI MANGIARE
15 NESPOLA 15

LO STATO DI MANGIARE
20 UVA 20

LO STATO DI MANGIARE
25 CAFFÈ 25

LO STATO DI MANGIARE
30 MORA 30

LO STATO DI MANGIARE
40 PRUGNA 40

LO STATO DI MANGIARE
50 CAVOLO 50

LO STATO DI MANGIARE
60 LAURO 60

LO STATO DI MANGIARE
75 FRAGOLA 75

LO STATO DI MANGIARE
80 SEDANO 80

LO STATO DI MANGIARE
1 BROCCOLI E

LO STATO DI MANGIARE
1¼ PINOLO E

LO STATO DI MANGIARE
1½ CILIEGIA E

LO STATO DI MANGIARE
2 RAVANELLO E

LO STATO DI MANGIARE
2½ KAKI E

LO STATO DI MANGIARE
3 COTOGNA E

LO STATO DI MANGIARE
5 SPINACI E

Mangiare

Donald Evans loved to plan menus for meals to cook and share with friends. He decided that for Mangiare the government must be a round table, and that among its food stamps it would issue pictorials named for things he saw listed on restaurant menus in Florence. But instead of making cookbook-type illustrations, he painted Italian landscapes and named them with puns on Italian dishes, which he imagined were the specialties of the different places he had painted.

In this series are views of the Lago Divinorosso, the Lake of Red Wine; Contorno, the hill town called Side Dish; S. Fagiolo in Olio, the church of St. Haricot Bean in Oil, with the holy bean on its shield; Castello Pisello, Pea Castle, with the royal pea on its shield; the Oceano Panifico, Baker's Ocean; Finnochiona and Mortadella, two landscapes named after special sausages; and the river town Funghi alla Greca, Pickled Mushrooms.

Donald Evans painted some of the stamps in colors that suggest the food and rubber-stamped them all with Mangiare's postmark and an overprint. He imagined that enemy Antipasto forces had used Mangiare's stamps during their wartime occupation of the country.

1944. Gastronomic landscapes. Occupation issue. Stamps of 1936-42 overprinted in black. (1974)

Between the wars, when commercial air travel was new, dirigibles became a craze. They were faster, quieter and more comfortable than planes; they traveled great distances without refuelling and could cross the Atlantic in three days. Their enormous gas bags had great lifting power, so the airships' gondolas were big enough to include dining rooms, lounges, promenades, passenger accommodations and crew quarters, as well as freight — a whole liner in the sky, complete with an onboard post office.

Donald Evans was fascinated by these airships and the old stamps that were issued specially for dirigible mail. He imagined that many of his own countries had their own airships, including Mangiare with its own giant phallic Cetriolo, the Cucumber. These four views show the majestic dirigible heading out over the Lago Divinorosso escorted by a wheeling biplane on the three etti and floating over the landscape on the five. On the one kilogram Il Cetriolo is visiting Pasta Asciutta (literally, Dry Pasta — pasta that has been cooked and drained), a region of Mangiare whose own stamps are on page 127. At the end of a flight, on the two kilogram, the Cetriolo is nosing into its moorings over a crowd of spectators at its huge home hangar at Giardino, the Garden.

Donald Evans wanted to have the originals of these dirigible stamps reproduced on a postcard to announce an exhibition, but before they could be photographed, they disappeared from the printing house, perhaps in the pocket of an overzealous collector of rare zeppelin stamps. He entered the loss in his catalogue as ''whereabouts unknown,'' and painted this second series, with the date of issue, 1927, added.

1927. Airpost. Reissue of the dirigible Il Cetriolo with added date inscription. (1974)

LO STATO DI MANGIARE
1927
POSTE AEREA
3 E.
IL CETRIOLO SURVOLANDO
IL LAGO DI VINOROSSO

LO STATO DI MANGIARE
1927
POSTE AEREA
5 E.
IL CETRIOLO

LO STATO DI MANGIARE
1927
POSTE AEREA
1 K
IL CETRIOLO SURVOLANDO
PASTA ASCIUTTA

LO STATO DI MANGIARE
1927
POSTE AEREA
2 K
IL CETRIOLO
AL GIARDINO

My Bonnie

"My Bonnie lies over the ocean." The [ALBEE 15 APR 76 MY BONNIE] phrase from the song meant America to Donald Evans, expatriate in Amsterdam. On a trip to New York in 1976 he visited the New York Horticultural Society Library and began the stamps for My Bonnie. Each peach, apple, pear, plum and cherry is taken from a real variety that he found illustrated in the plates of the encyclopedic studies published by the New York Agricultural Experiment Station at the turn of the century.

Donald Evans loved the variety and voluptuousness of the fruits' names and shapes, colors and volumes, from the blushing fullness of the peaches to the red-black dots of the cherries. He imagined that My Bonnie issued a horizontal row of each series, six stamps of five fruits, every year from 1962 to 1967. In each series he arranged the varieties randomly on the background colors of a cascading rainbow to create, he hoped, "a very fruitlike effect." My Bonnie is a dream of abundance.

It is also a country of friendship. When he found a fruit with the same name as a friend, Donald Evans would make a special stamp for his bonnie friend: Diana, Jonathan, Marie-Louise and Mother. He carved out a rubber eraser postmark for the capital which he called Albee, after his friend Edward Albee who had given him the country's name. And for the Museum of Modern Art he made a Christmas card for 1977 from My Bonnie with red and green stamps of holly and mistletoe.

1962-67. Peaches. (1976)

1962-67. Apples. (1976)

1962-67. Pears. (1976)

1962-67. Plums. (1976)

1962-67. Cherries. (1976-77)

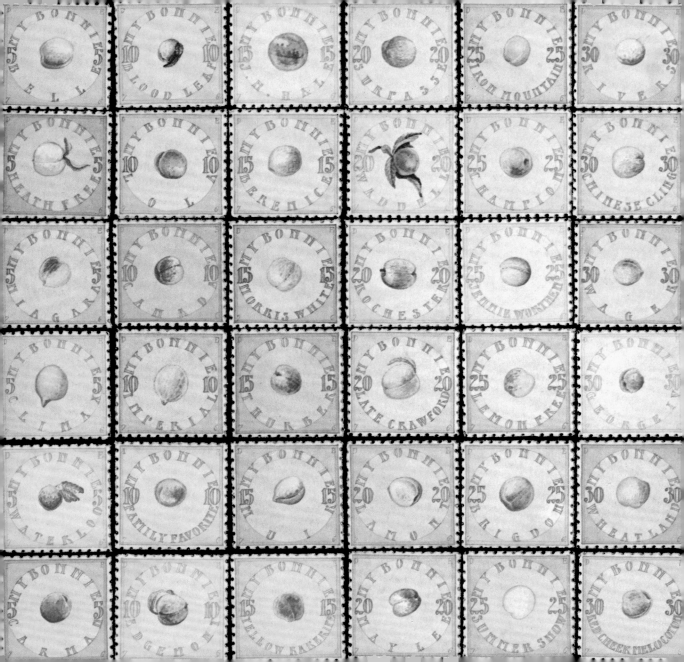

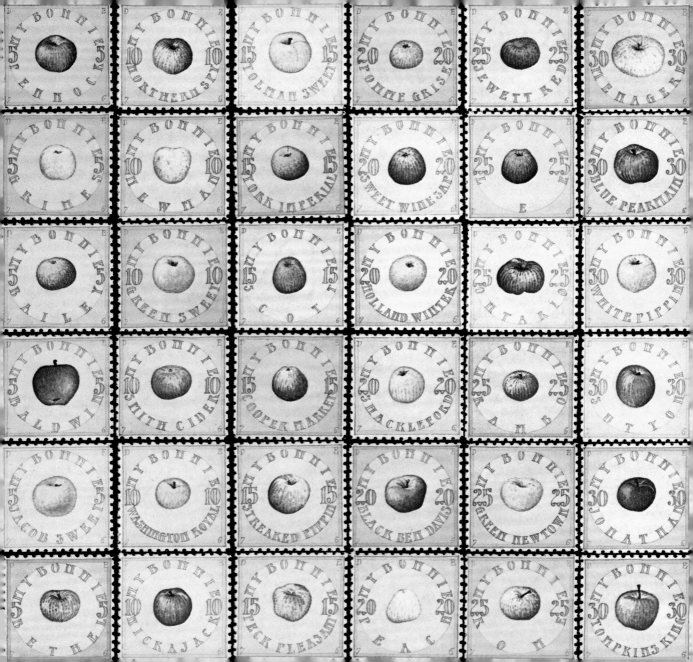

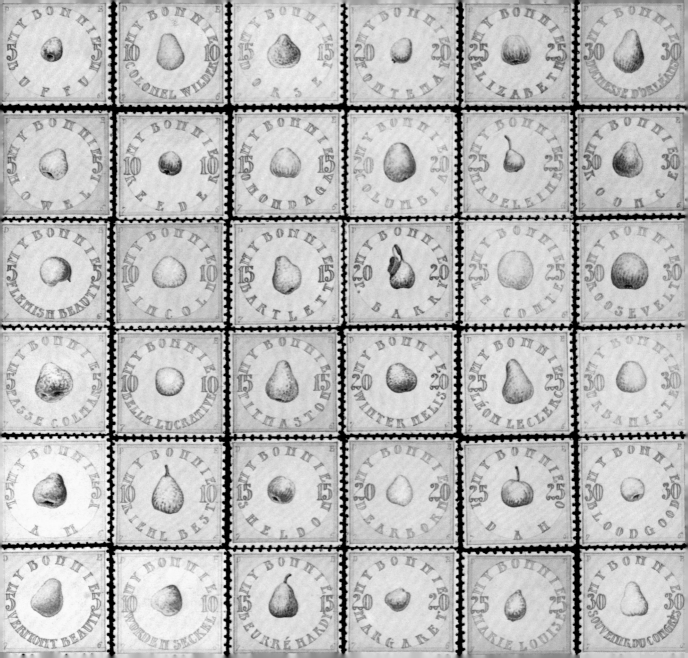

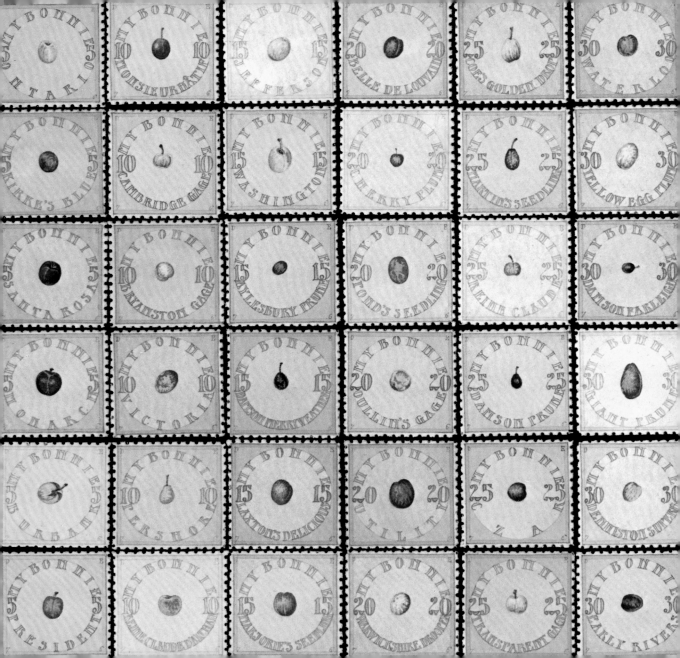

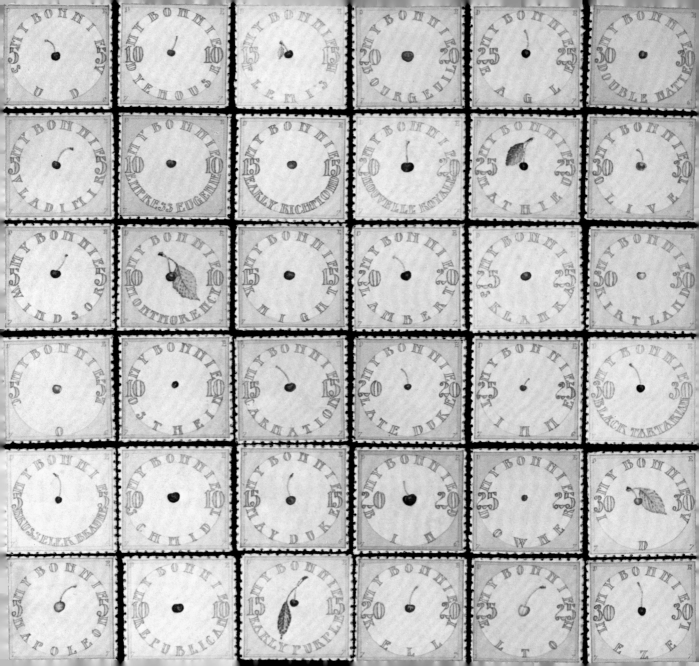

In colloquial Dutch, Nadorp means After ⬡ the Village, or on the other side of town. It is also the family name of a friend of ⬡ Donald Evans whom he honored as the ruler of this small country, Prince Philip ⬡ of Nadorp.

In this series, mounted on the back of an ⬡ envelope, he painted views of the coast. On the one stamp is a shallow marshy inlet with little tufts of islands, a view of the brackish swamp that was Holland before the dikes were built. The dam on the fifteen holds back the water from the fields and woods with the aid of a distant windmill. The odd pair of water towers on the two are built on flat reclaimed land to provide pressure for the flow of fresh water.

In this watery country the rise and fall of the tide marks the rhythm of the quiet days. On the three the tide has gone out, grounding a sailboat; on the five it is in, flooding the low marshes and driving the birds into the air.

Fishing is the local occupation: of the kite in flight on the ten, and of the men. The three boats are: an old-fashioned *botter* under sail on the twenty; and on the twenty-five and the fifty, two modern fishing boats with their nets out, one perhaps out after herring and the second a shrimper hauling in a catch of tiny pink *garnalen*.

Trailed by hungry sea gulls, they sail out from the shelter of broad deep harbors like Robertshaven on the thirty, through the even broader outlets to the sea on the twelve, past the coastal islands like that on the seventy-five, to fish the cold rough waters of the North Sea.

1938. Pictorials. Issued to propagandize the coastal provinces. (1976)

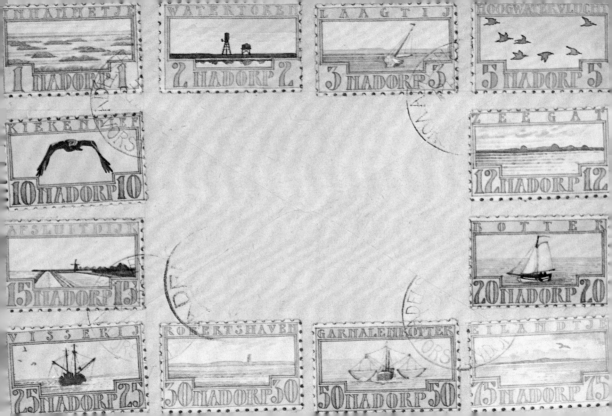

For the stamps of Nadorp, Donald Evans chose many subjects that are typically Dutch. As he did for Achterdijk, he made series of windmills, and in these twenty monochromes he repeated some of the ones on page 35. The standard of Nadorpsche currency is one hundred Buis to one Janssen, named after two of Donald Evans' friends.

He created playful place names for this imaginary country, made up from names of friends and regular Dutch words. On the coast are Robertshaven (Robert's Harbor) with its two windmills on the two Buis and the twenty-five Buis stamps, Afsluitdijk (the great dike that closes off the IJsselmeer from the North Sea) on the twenty, and Vissersdorp (Fishing Village) on the seventy-five; inland are Knuffelberg (Cuddle Hill) on the five, Philipsburg (Philip's Town) on the six, ten and ninety, Grotermeer (Greater Lake) on the seven and Boerderij (Farmhouse) on the eight.

Adelshoeve (Noble Farm) with its three windmills on the one, nine and twelve, is the capital Donald Evans chose for Nadorp; Alhier on the two means Local, or In the Neighborhood; Enkele on the fifty means One-way; and the last stamp, the one Janssen, he called Afgelopen (Over and Done).

Equally Dutch are the staple vegetables that are seen in every country kitchen garden, a typical miller's family fare: white cabbage, endive, head lettuce, red cabbage, escarole, Brussels sprouts, cauliflower and savoy cabbage; turnip, parsnip, carrot, radish, celery root, beet, potato and salsify. He set these mundane greens and roots floating like strange creatures on pale green and earth colored grounds.

Donald Evans liked Dutch village fairs and festivals and invented three celebrations for Dutch vegetables. He later made special vegetable souvenir sheets for anniversaries of the royal carrot harvesters, the royal cauliflower growers, and the royal potato peelers.

1953. Windmills. (1977)

1961. Vegetables. (1975)

1963. Root vegetables. (1975)

Raap — NADORP 10

Witte Peen — 15 NADORP

Wortel — NADORP 20

Radijs — NADORP 25

Knolselderij — NADORP 30

Biet — NADORP 35

Aardappel — NADORP 50

Schorseneer — NADORP 60

When Donald Evans was in America he painted American apples on the stamps of My Bonnie; when he was in Holland he painted Dutch apples on the stamps of Achterdijk and Nadorp. This envelope is the first of a dozen he made in Amsterdam in 1976, each with stamps of four different Nadorpsche apples mounted in the corners. These stamps show Bramley's seedling, the Charlamovsky, the double bellefleur and the tulip apple.

Each envelope is unaddressed and canceled five times; each bears a blue sticker, printed and perforated; and a white sticker drawn in red and rubber-stamped in black by Donald Evans, which indicates that this is the eighteenth registered letter sent from the post office in the capital of Adelshoeve in 1961. The other eleven envelopes are dated, one per year, through 1972.

Each stamp has a frame in three values of the same color with a multicolored apple highlighted against a circle of the darkest color. In the corners each stamp has the currency value of five, Donald Evans' favorite number.

286.

R ADELSHOEVE
196118

Nog te betalen means still to pay in Dutch. These are the postage-due stamps of Nadorp, the stamps the post office puts on letters without sufficient postage and asks to be paid for on delivery.

Like the ciphers of Adjudani, they are an abstract study in varying colors and shapes within the regular rhythm of circles in squares, here arranged in a grid. In his sketchbooks Donald Evans often played with the printing of the alphabet and numbers, and he liked to collect sets of rubber stamps in different typefaces. Soon after he began to paint his stamps in Holland he arrived at his style of outlined open letters over simple printing. He continued to refine and experiment with his letters, making the forms taller or shorter, thicker or thinner for the frames of various shapes that he laid out on his stamps.

This is the most elaborate set of Arabic numbers he designed, with the curling crossbar of the four, the broad swelling downstroke of the seven, the overlapping of the digits in the multiples of ten; it also appears in an adapted form on the windmills of Nadorp.

1942. Postage due. Ciphers. (1975)

As a child, Donald Evans took piano lessons and on his childhood stamps he had painted instruments and composers, especially the post horn and Chopin. He was moved by all kinds of music, from Glenn Gould's Mozart to the popular Egyptian singer Umm Kulthum; and he had many musician friends, for one of whom he made this special registered cover from Nadorp.

He had found a paperback book about old musical instruments and from its black and white illustrations he chose the ones whose shapes he liked: a melon-bellied lute with its bent-back pegbox; the long wooden curve and bell of an early *cor anglais;* an elegant *trompe* (descendant of the post horn) with its circular brass coil; a cornet with its two coils mirrored, one for each valve; and a view from above of the interior of a harpsichord.

He sketched the layout of the stamps over their pictures in the book, including the print and denomination numbers for the stamps, and ruled the guidelines of a transfer grid. He made notations about color choices and details.

Then in pencil he outlined the instruments faintly on his own perforated sheets, tinted the backgrounds with watercolor wash, and painted in the instruments, complete with brass and wood reflections and the twenty-four black keys on each of the harpsichord's two keyboards.

In the spring, Dutch people used to go out into the fields to gather little, speckled plovers' eggs (on the ninety here) from the birds' camouflaged nests. At home they would boil them for a moment, peel them, flatten them slightly between the palms and serve this delicacy with salt, fresh pepper and celery seed. Donald Evans loved them.

For the first issue of Fauna and Flora he had painted a series of eggs of native birds from postcards published by the Natural History Museum in London. Later he bought and studied books about birds' eggs and nests to learn their various patterns and shapes, and in April of 1977 did this almost luminescent set, which he called his Easter eggs, from the country of Nadorp.

He imagined the stamps were "issued to propagandize the Royal Bird Park at Adelshoeve," the capital, and listed the birds' English names in his catalogue: 1 Buis, mocking-bird; 2 B., robin; 3 B., little crake; 4 B., sooty tern; 5 B., ringed plover; 6 B., spotted redshank; 7 B., hooded crow; 8 B., quail; 9 B., fork-tailed flycatcher; 10 B., song thrush; 12 B., scissor-bill; 15 B., nightjar; 20 B., Cetti's warbler; 25 B., pheasant; 30 B., greenshank; 35 B., squacco; 50 B., gray-breasted rail; 60 B., Sabine's gull; 75 B., waterhen; 90 B., lapwing (whose eggs are commonly called plovers' eggs); 1 Janssen, kestrel; 1 J. 25, pennant-wing nightjar; 1 J. 50, Eleonora's falcon; 2 J., hobby; 2 J. 50, fairy tern; 3 J., pin-tailed sandgrouse; 5 J., dotterel; 10 J., pheasant-tailed jacana; 15 J., sparrowhawk; 20 J., jackdaw.

1969. Eggs of wild birds. (1977)

At dawn and dusk birds wade in the shallow ditches between the Dutch fields, eyeing the water, waiting to bob their long beaks down to catch their dinner.

Donald Evans made this first day of issue *(eerste dag van uitgifte)* envelope and stamps to commemorate the World Waders Conference held at Adelshoeve in the first week of spring, 1962. He painted the night heron, the little bittern, the bittern, and the heron on this perforated strip with a special commemorative plate inscription and plate number. A Buis is the cent of the Nadorpsche currency, so Buispost means penny post.

He also made many *luchtpost* (airmail) stamps for the *vorstendom* (principality) from photographs of early airplanes. He told the *Paris Review* that he imagined the postcard was a souvenir from one of Nadorp's first airmail flights. The image on the postcard is of a biplane's emergency landing in a grassy Dutch field. He liked to think the stamps had been mounted on the postcard, mailed on one of the early flights, and later sold as a curiosity to a collector. The stamps, from two different series, are three 1919 monochromes and a 1921 with a black biplane.

The first *kunstvlucht* (literally art flight, or stunt flight) in Nadorp Donald Evans imagined took place at the *vliegveld* (airfield) of Adelshoeve in the summer of 1924. He showed a Blackburn Ripon biplane doing a loop-the-loop on the eight stamps of a perforated sheet. It is neatly canceled with one centered postmark.

1962. World Waders Conference at Adelshoeve. Wading birds of Nadorp. (1973)

1922. Airpost of 1919 and 1921 on souvenir postcard. (1974)

1924. Stunt-flying. Block of eight stamps in souvenir sheet. (1976)

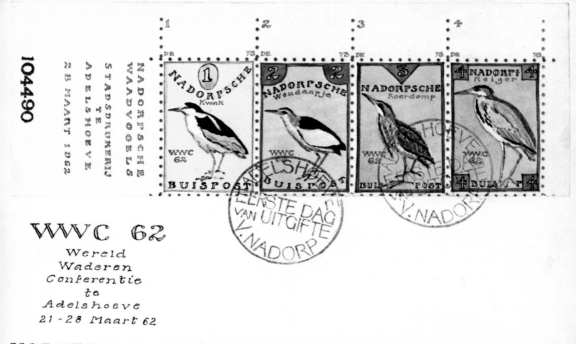

Dutch is a difficult language, and since most Dutchmen speak several other languages as well, they take it as a great compliment when foreigners learn the native tongue.

When he moved to Holland, Donald Evans decided to learn Dutch and these bright stamps were his vocabulary lessons, his way of learning common nouns. He made twenty-two horizontal sets of five stamps each, two images per stamp, which he dated one for each year from 1952 to 1973. He called them children's issues, following the example of the Dutch post office, which puts out special children's stamps.

The meanings of the words on these six horizontal sets are: gull/arrow, beehive/gear, leg/knife, kite/period, magnet/lute; stamp/rain, curtain/plate, nail/pyramid, glass/dog, sunrise/comma; grass/room, letter/sun, rainbow/kettle, canary/bicycle, roof/needle; ball of string/bridge, letter/fog, match/tulip, fork/bell, sunset/circle; stripe/wheel, necklace/cube, question mark/sock, globe/window, bowtie/rabbit; spoon/number, shaving brush/screw, package/ball, bottle/shadow, button/fly. The two Dutch genders are distinguished by *het* (the) for the neuter and *de* (the) for the "common," the merged masculine and feminine.

Apparently matched arbitrarily, they are everyday words for things to wear, shapes, parts of buildings, punctuation marks, the weather. Their images are laid out like a rebus, and many of them are found elsewhere in his work, especially, of course, the postage stamp, framed here in a stamp in a stamp. He painted the stamp in a stamp on other occasions, for a Christmas card to a friend and for a souvenir sheet commemorating his own World Philatelists' Congress at Adelshoeve in 1967.

1966, 1967, 1968, 1969, 1971, 1972. Children's issues. Vocabulary lesson. (1972, 1973)

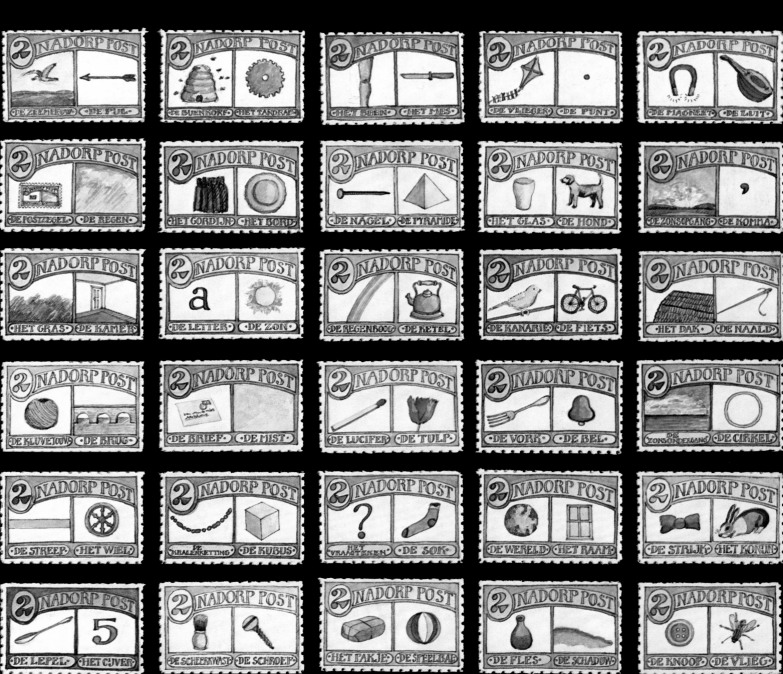

Pasta, a part of Mangiare, is an autono- mous region composed of twenty-five provinces, each boasting an example of its namesake noodle on its official coat of arms. Lasagne al Forno (Baked Lasagne or Lasagne on the River Forno) is the capital; its pasta is a green dough made with spinach and cut in broad ribbons.

In the provinces, there are differences in shape, from the baroque shell of Conchigilia and the butterfly of Farfalla to the simple strand of Spaghetto and the dot of Puntina. The stars of Stelle and Stellina, the weeds of Gramigna and Gramignona differ in size. A dumpling may be plain (Gnoccho) or stuffed with a surprise (Sorpresa). A tube designed to soak up a sauce may be textured with straight ribs (Pipa Rigata) or spirals (Tortiglione), or just plain (Chiffero). And finally, there are pastas for different occasions from the everyday Maccherone (Italian for Blockhead) to the festive doughnut-shaped Tortellone.

Pasta, especially fettuccine, was one of Donald Evans' favorite dishes. On a trip to Florence in the spring of 1974 he learned the names and shapes of many new varieties which he celebrated with this new country and its stamps.

1946. Arms of the provinces of Pasta. (1974)

When he was a child, Donald Evans had been moved by the magic dust of butterfly wings to paint several series of butterfly stamps which he had imagined were issued by the Central Lincolnian Federation, one of his American countries, in honor of its Butterfly Congresses.

Rups means Caterpillar in Dutch. Donald Evans invented this country at the request of his friend William Katz to commemorate the world première of a dance called "Caterpillar" with choreography by Louis Falco, music by Luciano Berio and décor and costumes by William Katz, performed in The Hague on February 18, 1975. Reproduced on the last page of the theater program was an express envelope with his first four stamps from Rups, two each of a nameless butterfly and caterpillar.

Later that year he studied more about butterflies and painted more accurate ones for Rups. He imagined that they were issued by the Rupische Posterijen (Rups' post office) and carved a postmark dated 11 Feb 75 with which he canceled them. His beginner's list of *rhopalocera* includes (in order by value) the Brimstone, the Southern White Admiral, Fenton's Wood White, the Pigmy Skipper, the Spanish Chalk-hill and the Turquoise Blues, the Ilex and the Moroccan Hairstreaks, the Large Copper, the Mediterranean Tiger Blue, the Gray Sooty Satyr, Martin's Blue, the Scarce Swallowtail and the Manto Ringlet.

1962. Butterflies. (1975)

Sabot

In French, *sabot* means wooden shoe, the typical wet-weather footwear worn in Holland and the marshier parts of France. Donald Evans had a Swedish pair that he wore on a trip to Paris (where there is a Rue du Sabot). At the time they were still exotic in that city, and people admired his. When he invented a French country, lying south of his Dutch countries, he named it after his shoes and called the capital Deuxfois (Twice) to make the pair. He thought of it as being like Belgium, a French kingdom with a northern culture.

In his notes for *Postcards to Gopshe,* he said Sabot was a country of noise and industry, mechanized by windmills, like the ones he saw on the highway from Amsterdam to Paris. Inspired by them, he painted his first series of windmills for his first show in Paris. He learned their structure from the color photographs in a Dutch book he had, and he used French for the stamp denominations. He varied the weather and time of day within frames that change shape in each column of stamps.

He gave the windmills the names of French, Dutch and American friends. Just as in the stamps of Achterdijk he had made his closest friends princes, here he gave their windmills the names of saints (a practice he took from the work of his friend Robert Indiana). He included his mother Dorothy as Dorothée, and his Paris dealers, Xiane and Eric, and a friend Dolores who he expected would see the show. Walter, the name of a Dutch friend, he decided to put in as a place in the north near the Dutch border. Happy to be showing his work in Paris, he called others by French words of greeting: Bon Jour, Accueil (Welcome), and Salut (Cheers). Accord (Harmony) he took from an upstate New York town whose name he loved.

1968. Windmills. (1974)

 SABOT — St. Remy — DEMI
 SABOT — Marilyn — UN
 SABOT — Xiane — DEUX
 SABOT — St. Phillipe — TROIS
 SABOT — Eric — QUATRE

 SABOT — Dorothee — CINQ
 SABOT — Sept Ponts — SIX
 SABOT — Dagmar — SEPT
 SABOT — Deuxfois — HUIT
 SABOT — Bonjour — NEUF

 SABOT — Accord — DIX
 SABOT — Salut — ONZE
 SABOT — Renard — DOUZE
 SABOT — Accueil — QUINZE
 SABOT — St. Guillaume — VINGT

 SABOT — Wallen — TRENTE
 SABOT — St. Michel — QUARANTE
 SABOT — Dolores — CINQUANTE
 SABOT — Cecile — SOIXANTE
 SABOT — Marandet — CENT

Wild mushrooms really must be learned from specimens found on hunts in the field with people who already know them. Illustrations are only a useful approximation, since individual variations are so great, and of course, a mistake can be fatal.

Donald Evans used to go on mushroom walks with knowledgeable friends and he became a dedicated collector of the edibles. Mushrooms are often camouflaged in their surroundings, difficult to spot, and his own very successful hunting technique was to crouch motionless and scan the landscape with his sharp eyes, rather than to march along looking. He said that he was pretending to be a mushroom, and he usually bagged more than anyone else.

To prepare for walks he also studied mushrooms in books, and from the illustrations in one of his books he painted two series of stamps. The top eight he imagined came first, "issued to stimulate public interest in foraging." and the second eight, unfortunately, came as an afterthought the following year, "to acquaint the foraging public with the most prevalent inedible species in an effort to prevent possible poisonings."

The common edible mushrooms include some of the tastiest and easiest to identify: the morel, the cepe, the meadow mushroom, the chanterelle, St. George's tricholoma, the delicious lactarius, and two russulas: the bare-toothed and the cracked green. The poisonous ones include some of the most deadly, as well as some most easily confused with the best edibles by a beginning collector.

1966. Edible mushrooms. (1973)

1967. Poisonous mushrooms. (1973)

Stein is the name of a picturesque village on the Maas River in the province of Limburg, the southeastern panhandle of Holland that lies between Belgium and Germany. Donald Evans went there on a visit with a friend in 1972; when he got back to Amsterdam he made a series of a dozen pictorials to commemorate the trip and to celebrate another part of his adopted country.

The stamps, in order by value, show: the view from Ulestraten, across the rolling hills; mushroom cultivation in caves; spotted cows at pasture; a view of the productive coal mines; haystacks by a roadside; a windmill in the countryside; a half-timbered barn; a distant view of the provincial capital of Maastricht; the chalk caves, from which comes a stone that hardens by itself in the air; a country road reminiscent of Donald Evans' first Achterdijk landscape; the regular rows of a poplar woods near Maastricht; and an architectural detail of a typical local wall laid in alternate courses of white stone and red brick, a style of building called *speklagen* (bacon layering) after its resemblance to bacon's stripes of fat and meat.

1955. Pictorials. (1972)

 STEIN 1c — GEZICHT VAN ULESTRATEN

 STEIN 2c — VERBOUWING VAN CHAMPIGNONS

 STEIN 3c — GRAZENDE KOEIEN

 STEIN 4c — GEZICHT OP DE MIJNEN

 STEIN 5c — HOOIBERGEN LANGS DE WEG

 STEIN 6c — EEN MOLEN IN HET PLATTELAND

 STEIN 8c — EEN PLAATSELIJKE SCHUUR

 STEIN 10c — GEZICHT OP MAASTRICHT

 STEIN 15c — MERGEL GROTTEN

 STEIN 20c — EEN WEG OP HET PLATTELAND

 STEIN 25c — HET BOS VÓÓR MAASTRICHT

 STEIN 50c — EEN MUUR VAN STEKLAGEN

One of Donald Evans' favorite writers was Gertrude Stein. When he made up the particulars of the country of Stein for his catalogue, he made her a kind of patron saint. He called the capital Gertrude Stein and the unit of currency a Gertrude of one hundred cents. The government is a literary dictatorship, which he imagined had educated the population to one hundred percent literacy. In his notes for *Postcards to Gopshe,* he said that everything is always being written down in Stein.

He celebrated his interest in the writer by making stamps with passages from her work printed in open letters. The top five he said were the type of 1964, the fiftieth anniversary of the publication of Stein's *Tender Buttons* from which the lines come. The stamps quote in full some of her shorter essays, obliquely descriptive, from the section called "Food," one of his favorite subjects too.

The block of four is dated 1972, the year Donald Evans made it and the fiftieth anniversary of "A Valentine to Sherwood Anderson." The beautiful passage he copied out is the section called "Let Us Describe," a description of a difficult imaginary journey. (He had a well-worn recording of Gertrude Stein reading this piece.) Donald Evans used his own Amsterdam postmark on these stamps in playful enjoyment of the coincidence that another Donald Evans, an American poet, had first published *Tender Buttons* in 1914.

1972. Gertrude Stein. *Tender Buttons* by Gertrude Stein. Type of 1964. (1972)

1972. Fiftieth anniversary of "A Valentine to Sherwood Anderson" by Gertrude Stein. (1972)

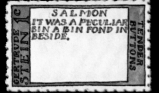

SALMON

IT WAS A PECULIAR
BIN A BIN FOND IN
BESIDE.

GERTRUDE STEIN 1¢ · TENDER BUTTONS

CHICKEN

ALAS A DIRTY WORD
ALAS A DIRTY THIRD
ALAS A DIRTY THIRD
ALAS A DIRTY BIRD

GERTRUDE STEIN 2¢ · TENDER BUTTONS

VEAL

VERY WELL. VERY WELL.
WASHING IS OLD,
WASHING IS WASHING.
COLD SOUP, COLD SOUP
CLEAN AND PARTICULAR
AND A PRINCIPAL.
A PRINCIPAL QUESTION
TO PUT INTO.

GERTRUDE STEIN 15¢ · TENDER BUTTONS

DINING

DINING IS WEST.

GERTRUDE STEIN 30¢ · TENDER BUTTONS

POTATOES

REAL POTATOES
CUT IN BETWEEN

GERTRUDE STEIN 1¢ · TENDER BUTTONS

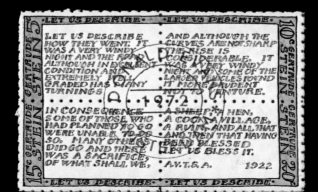

· LET US DESCRIBE · · LET US DESCRIBE ·

LET US DESCRIBE
HOW THEY WENT. IT
WAS A VERY WINDY
NIGHT AND THE ROAD
ALTHOUGH IN EXCELLENT
CONDITION AND
EXTREMELY WELL
GRADED HAS MANY
TURNINGS.

AND ALTHOUGH THE
CURVES ARE NOT SHARP
THE RISE IS
CONSIDERABLE. IT
WAS A VERY WINDY
NIGHT AND SOME OF THE
LARGER VEHICLES FOUND
IT MORE PRUDENT
NOT TO VENTURE.

IN CONSEQUENCE
SOME OF THOSE WHO
HAD PLANNED TO GO
WERE UNABLE TO DO
SO. MANY OTHERS
DID GO AND THERE
WAS A SACRIFICE,
OF WHAT SHALL WE,

A SHEEP, A HEN,
A COCK, A VILLAGE,
A RUIN, AND ALL THAT
AND THEN THAT HAVING
BEEN BLESSED
LET US BLESS IT.

A.V.T.S.A.   1922

· LET US DESCRIBE · · LET US DESCRIBE ·

15¢ GERTRUDE STEIN 5¢ · 10¢ GERTRUDE STEIN 5¢ · 15¢ GERTRUDE STEIN 20¢

Donald Evans' world was for the most part transatlantic. He lived on the East Coast of the United States and in Western Europe, and most of his imaginary countries lie in those parts of the world. But when he found a more exotic subject that interested him, he made up a country to issue stamps about it.

With Sung-Ting, the interest was Chinese ceramics. He studied them in books and museums and collected a few inexpensive later pieces, but those of the Sung dynasty (960-1280 A.D.) were his favorites. He loved them for their classic simplicity of color and shape, particularly Ting-yao (Ting ware), which was made at Ting Chou under imperial patronage in white, the Chinese color of mourning.

Donald Evans chose as the national emblem of Sung-Ting a plain Ting ware plate with its characteristically darker, unglazed rim. In his notes for *Postcards to Gopshe*, Donald Evans said the plate was on display in the national museum of art treasures in the capital city Lueh. For this work he painted the abstract shape in ten subdued colors in three series that indicate the country's postal history. The ten imperforate are Sung-Ting's first postage stamps; the second ten mark the introduction of the perforating machine; and the third show a growing Western influence with the Arabic numbers printed over the bottom Chinese numeral to make them "bilingual." The characters left and right of each circle read Sung-Ting, and the corners bear his signature: DE 76.

1880. Ting-yao. Arms of Sung-Ting. (1976)

1884. Ting-yao. Arms of Sung-Ting. Type of 1880. (1976)

1893. Stamps of 1884 overprinted in black. (1976)

Donald Evans spelled Sung-Ting in several ways on the country's stamps. When the name appeared in Roman letters, he spelled it Song-Ting to make a French transliteration, since he imagined French was the international diplomatic language used by the republic's post office. Here he changed the Chinese character for ting, which appears in the lower left corner of each stamp. This ting is an ancient Chinese ritual vessel, and it is also one of the hexagrams, The Cauldron, in the *I Ching,* the Chinese *Book of Changes,* which Donald Evans used to consult. The characters on the right side of each stamp read airmail.

In his notes for *Postcards to Gopshe,* he said Sung-Ting was a vast country of courteous and industrious people. Air service linking the sometimes-dangerous interior with the coast was inaugurated in 1928, and for the first airmail issue he painted twenty-four different-colored stamps with one or the other of two biplanes. He made them all five cents (one hundred cents equals one Sung-Ting dollar), as if the post office had taken the numeral 5 as a decorative element. Then he arranged the stamps to make a rhythmic dance of mosquitolike planes and overprinted Western numbers (except on the five) to make a range of values.

1928. Airpost. Shades of five cent values surcharged in black. (1975)

In 1971 Donald Evans spent a hot summer evening sitting talking and smoking marijuana with friends during a weekend party in the Catskills. Someone said, "It's so hot, it feels like the tropics," and the little group began to play with the word until it evolved into Tropides, the name they imagined for a lush little group of Caribbean islands.

When he returned to New York, Donald Evans made three stamps from the Tropides Islands to commemorate that evening, and in Holland in 1972 he took up the country again. He invented the geography of the archipelago and named its places after that weekend party.

He imagined the hot and humid islands lay in three groups. The Greater Trops are the two northernmost islands. Grand Trop (literally, Big Too Much in French) is an extinct volcano whose peak Chase Mountain is named after a mountain near the house in the Catskills. Doveman, a friend's nickname, became the capital of the archipelago. To the south lies haunted Lula Cay, named after the ghost in the Catskills house (*lula* means squid in Portuguese). The uninhabited Mid Trops consist of two large bald rocks called Monk's Head; in the Lesser Trops are two flat islands Pussy, and Michael's Ear, the latter named for Donald Evans' friend Michael Malcé. Jolie, the town on Michael's Ear, is named for Michael's wife, Jolie Kelter.

Donald Evans had painted many views of the islands (like the stamps on this book's cover) before Richard Marshall asked him to make a piece for a show called "Maps" at the Museum of Modern Art in New York in 1977. For the occasion, he mapped the islands on strips of stamps and mounted them on a registered envelope that he canceled with a special tourism promotion postmark: "Come to the Tropides, Isles of Beauty."

1965. Map of the Tropides Islands.

1965. Airpost. Map of the Tropides Islands. Inscribed with inter-island route of the Tropides Air Service. (1977)

Although he showed French and Portuguese influence in the islands' names, Donald Evans chose English as the official language of the Tropides and imagined that this black nation was a self-governing dominion with a parliament that met in Government House, the old white Georgian capitol in Doveman. He named the currency after Merle Peek, his host in the Catskills (one hundred Merles equal one Peek) and made up an economy based on tropical cash crops like Sea Island cotton, bananas, coconuts and coffee. The national coat of arms bears a Tropidesian palm.

In the four allegorical landscapes Donald Evans painted coral-based Lula Cay with a palm and Grand Trop with a coffee tree to symbolize the two islands' main crops. He designed each stamp with a tree centered in the foreground as if it were an architectural support to the wide straight frame. The composition is his variation on the "Oasis Theater," a favorite construction by his friend Cletus Johnson, the artist who makes scaled-down façades of imaginary theaters.

Donald Evans designed the palm stamps on the registered souvenir envelope as one perforated panoramic strip. Later he tore them apart, mounted them in the envelope's corners and added two printed stickers, his own Lula Cay registration label and five cancellations — four from the Lula Cay post office where the envelope was mailed and one from the Doveman post office on Grand Trop. This piece of airmail was evidently routed through the capital to be transferred to an international flight for dispatch to the outer world.

1958. Pictorials. (1976)

1930. Allegorical landscapes. (1975)

1960. Palms. (1973, 1974)

TROPIDES ISLANDS
3ᵐ BANANA BLOW-DOWN

TROPIDES ISLANDS
5ᵐ TRAVELLER'S PALM

TROPIDES ISLANDS
10ᵐ COCONUT GROVE

TROPIDES ISLANDS
15ᵐ CROSS ISLAND ROAD

TROPIDES ISLANDS
25ᵐ THE LAKE

TROPIDES ISLANDS
35ᵐ GRAND TROP

TROPIDES ISLANDS
50ᵐ COPRA HANGING TO DRY

TROPIDES ISLANDS
60ᵐ SCHOONER

In search of new subjects, Donald Evans made encyclopedic studies of fruits and plants. The orchard stamps of My Bonnie were one result and a palm garden of the Tropides was another.

Like the penguins on page 77, he painted them in pastel colors, set them in nichelike frames, and organized them from the dwarf palmetto on the ½ Merle (its trunk grows half underground) to the majestic royal palm on the 10 Peek. In between, he included specimens with palmate or pinnate (feathered) fronds; their trunks are smooth-ringed or crosshatched, straight or curved, bulbous or spindly. This is the first of two series, forty different palms in all.

Another of Donald Evans' studies of nature's variety are the shells of the Tropides. The scientific names were too long to be put on the stamps, but he listed them in his Catalogue of the World: ½ Merle, *Calliostoma zizyphinum*; 1M., scallop: *Pecten nobilis*; 2M., sea snail: *Neverita josephina*; 3M., helmet: *Cassis cornuta*; 5M., cockle: *Venericardia antiquata*; 10M., *Fissidentalium vernedei*; 12M., *Hippopus hippopus*; 15M., conch: *Strombus gigas*; 20M., leopard cone: *Conus leopardus*; 25M., spider shell: *Lambis truncata truncata*; 30M., tiger cowrie: *Cypraea tigris*; 50M., *Codakia exasperata*; 1 Peek, *Cassidaria echiniphora*; 2P., pecten: *Chlamis farreri*; 3P., chambered nautilus: *Nautilus pompilius*; 5P., zebra volute: *Amoria zebra*.

He thought of these stamps as one work on four envelopes. Each is registered and postmarked at the post office of a different island, and all are airmail except the cover from Charlotte. (As the map on page 143 shows, Pussy Island is not on the inter-island route of the Tropides Air Service. It's too swampy for a runway.)

1949. Palms. (1976)

1959. Shells. (1974)

TROPIDES ISLANDS — DWARF PALMETTO — ½ POSTAGE

TROPIDES ISLANDS — FEATHERDUSTER PALM — 1 POSTAGE

TROPIDES ISLANDS — CHERRY PALM — 2 POSTAGE

TROPIDES ISLANDS — COHUNE PALM — 3 POSTAGE

TROPIDES ISLANDS — OVERTOP PALM — 5 POSTAGE

TROPIDES ISLANDS — SPLENDID PALM — 8 POSTAGE

TROPIDES ISLANDS — COCONUT PALM — 10 POSTAGE

TROPIDES ISLANDS — CABBAGE PALM — 12 POSTAGE

TROPIDES ISLANDS — WINDMILL PALM — 15 POSTAGE

TROPIDES ISLANDS — HAT PALM — 20 POSTAGE

TROPIDES ISLANDS — PETTICOAT PALM — 25 POSTAGE

TROPIDES ISLANDS — SEGUSI PALM — 35 POSTAGE

TROPIDES ISLANDS — THATCH PALM — 50 POSTAGE

TROPIDES ISLANDS — WAX PALM — 60 POSTAGE

TROPIDES ISLANDS — MANILA PALM — 75 POSTAGE

TROPIDES ISLANDS — SILVER PALM — 1 POSTAGE P

TROPIDES ISLANDS — SENTRY PALM — 2 POSTAGE P

TROPIDES ISLANDS — ROCK PALM — 3 POSTAGE P

TROPIDES ISLANDS — BARREL PALM — 5 POSTAGE P

TROPIDES ISLANDS — ROYAL PALM — 10 POSTAGE P

R CHARLOTTE
1 9 5 9 0 1

R JOLIE
1 9 5 1 0 1

PAR AVION

Donald Evans was fascinated by exotic fruit. Wherever he went, he was on the lookout for new kinds, especially at Chinese and Puerto Rican fruit stands in New York and the Indonesian stalls in Amsterdam. He was always experimenting with fruit salad.

He invented one country, Selamat Makan (the Indonesian phrase for Enjoy Your Dinner), just for East Indian fruits, and for the Tropides he painted four different series, all of tropical fruit. This is the second of the Tropides series, the brightest in color and the most elaborate in design.

In 1973, Donald Evans' friend Marisol was showing sculptures of tropical fish in New York. For the occasion he painted her a present of stamps from the country of Marisol with pictures of her fish in Spanish Baroque frames. Later that year, when he made these stamps for the Tropides, he designed their sixteen even more exotic frames. Then he played with the lettering: sometimes it is straight and sometimes curving; letters are elongated and words are split to fit them into and around the frame. Finally he laid out the piece in regular checkerboard squares.

He imagined that these stamps were issued by the Tropides Printing Office in Doveman "to propagandize the Tropides Islands experiment stations" (which were busy with palms as well as fruit). In the fourth and last of the series, Donald Evans showed the vast extent of the experiment stations' studies with a sheet of pastel monochromes of eighty-eight varieties of tropical fruit. In his notes for *Postcards to Gopshe,* he said the islanders lived on the fruit that fell from the trees.

Donald Evans collected old American quilts and coverlets. He liked their strong, bright colors; their abstract patterns; and their display of nimble-fingered, waste-not, want-not craft.

He had seen some of these quilts in the New York shop Kelter-Malcé which belongs to his friends Jolie Kelter and Michael Malcé, whom he had honored in the Lesser Trops. When the Whitney Museum of American Art had a quilt show in 1971, he bought the catalogue of the show and from it painted this series of stamps. Most of the original quilts were made in Pennsylvania in the second half of the nineteenth century, but Donald Evans imagined that they came from the Tropides, the country of his friends.

A pieced quilt is made of scraps of cloth that have been stitched together. On these stamps he painstakingly painted in the outlines of the pieces and their borders, just as he painted in the twill on the tartans of Antiqua. Over the simplest design, the Amish Stripes, he rubber-stamped his postmark for Grand Trop with its palm tree coat of arms and five-starred cross (one star for each island). He listed the names of the traditional patterns in his catalogue: Windmills, Log Cabin, Stripes, Bay Leaf, Rainbow, Wild Goose Chase, Tree Everlasting and Circles and Crosses.

1964. Tropidesian pieced quilts. (1972)

TROPIDES 2½

TROPIDES 5

TROPIDES 10

TROPIDES 15

TROPIDES 30

TROPIDES 35

TROPIDES 60

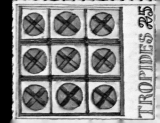

TROPIDES 25

The four chairs on these stamps were col- lected from the streets of New York by the illustrator Philippe Weisbecker as models for this work. Once when Donald Evans came to visit New York he bor- rowed the Weisbecker loft to live and work in.

The loft was near the Bowery, and had bare brick walls, a bare wood floor, a low bed, a table and the chairs, each uncomfortable and decrepit in a different way (like the very odd though handsome chairs that Donald Evans had once collected for his own equally bare Brooklyn apartment). At the end of his stay, as a thank-you, Donald Evans made a souvenir sheet, matted it, put the inscription "Welcome home" on the back, and hung it on the wall.

He made the country a principality and his friend the ruler. This issue he painted in bright, clear colors in honor of the National Chair Works, punning on the French for masterwork, chef d'oeuvre. The currency he named after his friend and his cat, one hundred Philos to one Weisbecker franc.

He carved the postmark for the capital which he called Vanupieds, or Barefoot Vagabond, a fair description of the way he tramped around the world, camping out and working in the homes of friends. The extra ten Philos he added to the stamps' face value at the bottom is standard philatelic practice with special souvenir sheets.

1973. National chairs. Block of four in souvenir sheet. (1973)

CᴵE ᴅᴇꜱ POSTES WEISBECKER

WEISBECKER WEISBECKER

WEISBECKER WEISBECKER

CHAISES ᴅᴏᴇᴜᴠʀᴇꜱ NATIONAUX

10•10ᴾᴴ

In Holland early in 1972, Donald Evans saw the Nederlands Dans Theater, the national modern dance company, per- form a new work called "Journaal." The choreography was by Louis Falco and the décor and costumes were by William Katz. Donald Evans' two American friends presented in the piece their impressions of Dutch life, performed by dancers dressed in the colors of the spectrum.

Donald Evans was enthusiastic about "Journaal," and he was particularly entranced by one of the leading dancers, Yteke Waterbolk. He described her as "a wonderful regal sort of young woman" with a wonderful name that sounded to him like Ithaca, his college town. He soon painted her por- trait from a photograph taken by a mutual friend, the Dutch painter Walter Nobbe. The portrait was the first stamp from a new country, a kingdom (*koninkrijk* in Dutch) named after Her Royal High- ness Queen Yteke.

Since childhood, Donald Evans' favorite real stamps had been early ones engraved with portraits of rulers, such as the old Dutch issues with Queen Wilhelmina on them. For his own stamps, he painted thirty-six portraits of his new friend Yteke in the colors of the rainbow, arranged in diagonals like the later stamps of My Bonnie.

When he entered this first perforated series from Yteke in his catalogue, Donald Evans gave the stamps various dates of issue. Following typical nineteenth-century practice, he imagined that a set of basic values was issued first and then the royal post office added stamps of other denominations as they needed them, such as the *anderhalf* (1½) and the higher values, distinguished in this series with gray-black frames. The standard of currency is one hundred ij to one IJ.

1878-96. Queen Yteke. Type of 1873. (1973)

158

Cold climates agreed with Yteke Waterbolk and Donald Evans imagined her country in the north of Europe. He traveled in Scandinavia and studied the north before he painted the sparsely populated landscapes of Yteke and the special quality of light in the northern skies.

The stamps on the envelope show typical Ytekan scenes: the River Lichaam (Body), spanned by the bridge at the capital, Stad Geest (Town of Soul); an iceberg; a gull in flight; a coastal steamer in pack ice; a parhelion over the sea; a glacier's edge where the icebergs are formed; a mirror-surfaced canal in Geest; a narwhal, or unicorn whale, with its spiraled ivory tusk; a waterfall; and a sunset at sea.

Donald Evans also invented a history for the country, which began in 1870 when the twin kingdoms of Lichaam and Geest (Body and Soul) united to become Yteke. As the country developed in his imagination, he made stamps to commemorate new provinces. He painted the pastel stamps with ice gray scenes for the twenty-fifth anniversary of the final expansion of Yteke's territories at the turn of the century. The stamps tell a short story of fishing life in the northern sea: a ship in port, Mount Edzo (named after Yteke Waterbolk's father), drift ice, shoving off from the drift ice, rowing, Mount Ida (one of Yteke's nicknames), auks, throwing the harpoon, rowing back to the ship, and the ship returning to port.

When the Lichaam and Geest stamps on page 91 were sold, Donald Evans made a new and larger series of northern animals, this time from Yteke. He varied each frame slightly in the corners around each animal: a barn owl, a beaver, a saddle-backed harp seal, a gray dolphin, a wolverine, a codfish, a polar bear, a kestrel, a limpet, a red deer, a boar, a hooded seal and a rook.

1970. Pictorials. Tourism promotion. (1974)

1926. Twenty-fifth anniversary of the opening of the Northern Territories. (1975)

1930. Fauna of Yteke. (1974)

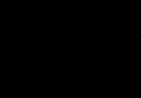

In 1922 Ytekan inland airmail service began. The first *luchtpost* (airmail) stamps show biplanes flying over Ytekan landscapes, and their values correspond to the distance from the aerodrome at Geest to the places on the stamps, the highest value and most distant place being the North Cape.

With the 1938 issue, Yteke began the practice of putting birds on its airmail stamps instead of flying machines. Donald Evans knew about the seabirds that live in huge colonies along the northern European coast and decided that the royal post office would honor them on this issue. He painted these six birds from photographs and placed them in pale seascapes in a pyramid of triangles.

On the fifteen ij the mute swan is flying along the distant winter coast of Ida. The common gull soaring on the twenty-five follows a fishing boat that Donald Evans drew from a photo of a Norwegian Royal Mail boat that he found in a children's book. The thirty-five ij has a swallow wheeling near a huge sea rock. The other birds are: a herring gull on the forty-five, a tern on the sixty and a great black-backed gull gliding on the ninety.

1938. Airpost. Sea birds and maritime landscapes. (1976)

For an earlier piece, Donald Evans had painted four stamps of northern landscapes and mounted them in the corners of an envelope as a present to Yteke Waterbolk on her birthday in February 1977. He had framed the cool, calm views of mountains and sea and clear pale skies under a broad prosceniumlike curve; he said he thought of them as portraits of her.

This second version shows three more views in frames of the same design and three possibilities for a fourth in progress. He sketched the scene and the lettering in pencil outline, and worked to balance the values on each rectangle as he finished them in watercolor and ink.

In an interview with *Quest* magazine, Donald Evans said watercolor "has a beauty and a beautiful luminosity and freshness to it, and if you try to labor it to fix something it goes flat and it looks awful.… It's really not a medium in which you can lie and cheat and try to fool people. That makes it very special."

If the unfinished stamps had turned out special, he would have chosen the one of the three *twintig ij* that worked best on the envelope and perhaps added a registered label to the composition. If he had liked the leftover stamps, he would have kept them to put in a new series or on an envelope as a present for a friend.

Donald Evans had already sent his new finished work to London for a show in the gallery of his friend Hester van Royen when he was working on these stamps. He planned to follow shortly for the opening. This piece was left unfinished when he died in a fire in Amsterdam on April 29, 1977.

Unfinished landscapes. (1977)

CHRONOLOGY

1945   Born Morristown, New Jersey, August 28

1952-61   Maintained stamp collection

1957-61   Painted c. 1,000 stamps for a fantasy world

1969   Bachelor of Architecture, Cornell University

1969-72   Architectural designer, construction and project supervisor, Richard Meier & Associates, Architects, New York

1972   To Schalkwijk (Utrecht); later to Amsterdam Began again to paint stamps for a fantasy world

1976   Visiting professor of art, University of North Carolina at Greensboro

1977   Died, Amsterdam, The Netherlands, April 29

ONE-MAN EXHIBITIONS

1972   Galerij Asselijn, Amsterdam

1973   Collection d'art/Galerie, Amsterdam

1974   Stedelijk Museum, Schiedam, The Netherlands
Galerie Germain, Paris
Hester van Royen Gallery, London
Gemeentemuseum, Arnhem, The Netherlands

1975   Fischbach Gallery, New York
Collection d'art/Galerie, Amsterdam
Galerie Germain, Paris

1976   Galerie Fenna de Vries, Rotterdam
Vick Gallery, Philadelphia
Fendrick Gallery, Washington
Fischbach Gallery, New York

1977   Hester van Royen Gallery, London

SELECTED GROUP EXHIBITIONS

1972   "Galerij Asselijn te gast." De Doelen, Rotterdam

"Najaarstentoonstelling." Galerie Fenna de Vries, Rotterdam

1973   "Mail Art." Kunsthistorisch Instituut der Universiteit van Amsterdam

1974   "Works on Paper." Virginia Museum, Richmond

"Artist's Stamps and Stamp Images." Traveling exhibition organized by Simon Fraser University, Burnaby, British Columbia

"Art on Paper." Weatherspoon Art Gallery, University of North Carolina at Greensboro

"Small Is Beautiful." Angela Flowers Gallery, London

1975   "Amsterdam koopt kunst." Stedelijk Museum, Amsterdam

"The Small Scale in Contemporary Art." Art Institute of Chicago

"Envelopes." J.P.L. Fine Arts, London

"Premier Salon de la Critique." Galerie de La Défense, Paris

1976   "Works in Miniature." Vick Gallery, Philadelphia

"Painting and Sculpture Today." Indianapolis Museum of Art

"Timbres et Tampons d'Artistes." Musée d'Art et d'Histoire, Geneva

"Collector's Gallery X." McNay Art Institute, San Antonio

"Art on Paper." Weatherspoon Art Gallery, University of North Carolina at Greensboro

1977   "Maps." Museum of Modern Art, New York

"Contemporary Pastels and Watercolors." Indiana University, Bloomington, Indiana

1978   "Artists' Postcards." Traveling exhibition under Smithsonian Institution auspices

1979   "Small Is Beautiful." Freedman Gallery, Albright College, Reading, Pennsylvania

"Directions." The Hirshhorn Museum and Sculpture Garden, The Smithsonian Institution, Washington, D.C.

"Reality of Illusion." Traveling exhibition organized by the Denver Art Museum, Denver, Colorado

Baker, Kenneth. "Review of Exhibitions: New York: Donald Evans at Fischbach." *Art in America* 63 (July-August 1975): 103.

Buckley, Tom. "About New York: 2 Artists in Flesh Tones." *New York Times* (April 7, 1975): 28.

Evans, Donald. "A Portfolio of Stamps of the World." *Paris Review,* no. 62 (Summer 1975): 75-87.

Fox, Howard. *Directions.* Smithsonian Institution Press, Washington, D.C. (1979): 23-24 and 82-84.

Frank, Peter. "New York Reviews: Donald Evans (Fischbach)." *Art News* 74 (Summer 1975): 136-37.

Gablik, Suzi. "Donald Evans, 1945-1977." *Art in America* 65 (July-August 1977): 14-15.

Gardner, Paul. "The Secret Kingdoms of Donald Evans." *Arts* magazine 49 (March 1975): 76-78.

Gruen, John. "On Art: Donald Evans." *Soho Weekly News* (April 3, 1975): 14.

Higgins, E. F., III. "Artists' Stamps." *The Print Collector's Newsletter* Vol. X No. 5 (November-December 1979): 154-156.

Katz, William. "Donald Evans." *Arts* magazine 51 (December 1976): 8.

Kotte, Wouter. "Stamp-Art: Alternatieve en Subtiele Kunstvorm."*Kunstbeeld* (May 1980): 16-19.

Mainardi, Pat. "Arts Reviews: Donald Evans." *Arts* magazine 51 (February 1977): 28.

Mastai, M. L. d'Otrange. *Illusion in Art.* Abaris Books, New York (1975): 362-364.

McKaughan, Molly. "Small Is Beautiful." *Quest* magazine (November-December 1977): 62-65.

Van Haaren, H. J. A. M. "Postzegels van de wereld van Donald Evans." *Catalogue Informatieblad Collection d'art/Galerie* (October-November 1975).

White, Paul William. "U.K. Reviews: Donald Evans at the Hester van Royen Gallery." *Studio International* 189 (January-February 1975): 12.

"Arts Without Letters. *Esquire* magazine (August 1973): 106-107.

"Donald Evans." *Avenue* (May 1973): 59 and 65-66.

"Postzegels uit de wereld van Donald Evans." *Informatieblad Gemeentemuseum Arnhem,* No. 58 (December 1974).

"The World of Donald Evans." *Cornell Alumni News* 80 (February 1978): 18-21.

List of Illustrations

All works are watercolor on paper reproduced actual size against black to simulate the philatelic stock sheets used by Donald Evans for display.

The text of this book was set by Johnson/Kenro, Inc., Freeport, New York, in ITC Garamond Book Condensed. Color separations were made from the original art by Princeton Polychrome Press, Princeton, New Jersey. The text stock is 80# Vintage Velvet manufactured by The Northwest Paper Company, Cloquet, Minnesota, and supplied by The Willco Paper Company, New York. The book was printed by Princeton Polychrome Press and bound by A. Horowitz and Sons, Fairfield, New Jersey.